MW01068117

Voluntary Ejaculation and Male Multiple Orgasms

Instruction Manual for Masculine Sexual Mastery

By Al Link and Pala Copeland

Photographs by Al Link and Pala Copeland.
Line drawings by Amanda Watters and Steve Copeland.

© **4 Freedoms Consulting LLC**

First Electronic Book Edition 2004
Revised Print Edition 2013
All rights reserved

ISBN 978-1-927498-10-1

Table of Contents

Introduction

"The degree and kind of a man's sexuality reach up into the ultimate pinnacle of his spirit." Friedrich Nietzsche – Beyond Good and Evil

Is this an all too familiar scenario? Hot and heavy loving with hungry kisses and tender caresses that promise orgasmic bliss for both you and your eager partner when all of a sudden you're one thrust past the edge, the dam bursts and it's over. You're finished, "spent" and ready for sleep. She's still waiting for more, perhaps wistfully contemplating a purchase of that acrylic-vibrating dildo her friend has been raving about.

Most ordinary men believe that ejaculation is the best part of sex. But there is something better— orgasms without any ejaculation at all. It is possible to have many orgasms in a single session of lovemaking, none of which includes an ejaculation. Furthermore, if you end lovemaking while you still have desire, in other words without ejaculating, you will super-boost your immune system and increase your physical energy, mental creativity, emotional resilience and spiritual quickening.

Orgasm and ejaculation are not the same thing. Using simple techniques that we explain here, any ordinary man can experience orgasms without ejaculating. Any male who learns how to do this will achieve alpha male status, radiating a masculine charisma that is irresistible to women. You do not already have to be a super-stud to learn how.

One of the best-kept secrets of our time is that **men (not just women) can be multi-orgasmic**. Not only

1

can a man have several orgasms during one session of lovemaking, but also he can do it and still have lots of energy and desire. The key is learning to separate orgasm from ejaculation. Because ejaculation follows orgasm so closely—within a split second—most people think they are one and the same, but they are two distinct phenomena. With the simple techniques explained in this book, you can learn to experience the pleasure of orgasm without the accompanying letdown of ejaculation.

There are **only two things you need to learn in order to become a multi-orgasmic man**, able to separate orgasm from ejaculation:

1. Stay relaxed no matter how sexually aroused you are.
2. Move your hot sexual energy up and away from your genitals.

Any man who does this and makes love long enough to build a very high sexual charge will eventually spontaneously experience non-ejaculatory orgasm.

Advantages of Voluntary Ejaculation

1. You can last as long as you want in active lovemaking, including during intercourse.
2. You can give your female partner complete sexual satisfaction by taking as long as she wants and needs to have all the orgasms she can stand.
3. Your relationship with your lover can be immeasurably enhanced and strengthened. She will adore you!
4. You can experience a great deal of physical pleasure, more than you could possibly imagine.
5. You can become a multi-orgasmic man, having any number of orgasms in a single session of lovemaking that extends over a period of hours.
6. Each orgasm can last longer and be more intense than an ordinary ejaculation. Usually these orgasms are experienced as pleasure throughout the body rather than being restricted to the genitals alone.
7. You can maintain optimal prostate health.
8. You can super-boost your immune system for total well-being, rarely getting sick and recovering quickly when you do.
9. You can experience a tremendous increase in available energy throughout each day.
10. You can have available a deep source of creativity to draw upon for application in all other areas of your life, for example, business, science, sports and the arts.
11. You can gain a serious competitive advantage over other ordinary males who do not know how to do this.

12. You can regularly experience states of sexual/spiritual ecstasy in which time stands still and the boundaries between you and your lover completely disappear.
13. You can regularly experience various forms of mystical altered states of consciousness.
14. You can radiate a sense of self-confidence and charisma that you formerly may have envied in other superior alpha males.

Three Types of Orgasm

When the Prince of Wales, later to be King Edward VII, said to his mistress, Lily Langtry, during a quarrel, that "I've spent enough on you to buy a battleship," she replied, "And you've spent enough in me to float one."

Ejaculation Orgasm

You have probably been regularly experiencing the pleasure of ejaculation since early adolescence. During an orgasm accompanied by ejaculation, a man's whole body tenses while contractions of the prostate gland vigorously propel semen out the tip of the penis in a forceful shooting stream. For a few seconds there is intense pleasure, restricted almost exclusively to the genitals. Almost immediately (usually within one or two minutes) the erection subsides and a refractory (recovery) period sets in. The entire body relaxes (not just the penis) and most men experience a complete loss of interest in further sexual activity. Sleepiness also commonly follows an ejaculation. How long it takes before energy (capacity for another erection) and libido (sexual desire) are restored depends on the man's age, health, and frequency of ejaculation. Some younger, stronger men are able to retain an erection in spite of ejaculation by maintaining rapid, continuous thrusting.

No matter how good it feels, repeated ejaculation with its accompanying loss of sexual energy can deplete your body's strength and vitality, and this is true for even the strongest, most virile males.

Prostate Ejaculation Orgasm

As you practice the techniques presented in this manual you may experience an **orgasm with prostate ejaculation**. This is noticeably different from a regular ejaculation. With a prostate ejaculation the contractions of the prostate are not as strong and a smaller quantity of ejaculate is expelled. The ejaculate dribbles out the end of the penis rather than shooting out in a forceful stream. The pleasurable sensation localized in your genitals will be less intense, but so will the resulting letdown and loss of physical energy. You will find that the refractory period is considerably shortened allowing you to more quickly regain another erection.

When you have a prostate ejaculation this is evidence that you are learning to keep the external genital muscles and the internal smooth muscles relaxed rather than involuntarily tensing them as in an ordinary ejaculation. It is a definite sign of progress on your journey toward masculine sexual mastery.

Non-Ejaculation Orgasm

A non-ejaculatory orgasm is as good as it gets. This is the best of both worlds. You get to have an orgasm, and you get to keep your erection and your sexual desire! Not only can you keep your erection for as long as your partner wants and needs to have all the orgasms she can stand, you can also go on to have any number of orgasms, with the intensity of each one varying from mild to overwhelming. You will be a multi-orgasmic man. **There is no greater physical pleasure than this.**

Three Types of Orgasm

You can accomplish this wondrous experience regularly by learning to stay completely relaxed regardless of how sexually aroused you become, by successfully circulating your hot sexual energy up through your body, away from the prostate, and by extending your active lovemaking over a period of hours.

As you learn the required skills your entire body will become an orgasmic erogenous zone. You may experience orgasmic sensations in your toes, for example, or rippling through your entire body rather than only in your genitals. There is no physical limit to how many of these energy orgasms you can have in a single session of lovemaking.

Rather than experiencing a physical letdown and loss of energy, you can build indefinitely to higher and higher energy intensity. Many men experience a mystical opening of the higher spiritual centers that far surpasses the extraordinary physical satisfaction of multiple orgasms. It is an experience beyond physical pleasure.

If you **end the lovemaking while you still have desire**, in other words with no ejaculation at all, you will build up a reserve of sexual energy that can be used to give you a powerful competitive advantage in any endeavor including sports, business, science or art. For thousands of years, Eastern emperors, princes and lords used this secret to accomplish greatness and rule their world. Even if you are not interested in leadership alpha male status, you can benefit from the tremendous boost in your immune system function, maintaining optimal vibrant health. And, active **male lovers who preserve their seed become highly attractive to women**.

During a non-ejaculatory orgasm, the physical pleasure will not travel out the end of your penis to be lost forever. Rather it will move through your entire body bathing every cell in the most exquisite sensations. Furthermore, while an ordinary ejaculation lasts merely seconds, the non-ejaculatory variety can go on for minutes and will sometimes result in such a delightfully altered state of consciousness that time simply becomes irrelevant and you enter into a continuous timeless bliss state. Your body may contract and jerk involuntarily with the force of this flow of ecstatic energy.

We hope that you are beginning to understand that **by not ejaculating you will not give anything up!** There is nothing to lose and so much to gain. After all, you can always have an ejaculation any time you want to, but most men who learn to have an orgasm without ejaculation usually experience ejaculation as a letdown that ends the pleasure and seriously depletes physical energy. By comparison, orgasms without ejaculation leave you relaxed, but not tired. You keep your erection or get another one as soon as you or your lover wants. You will still have intense desire and this will not be experienced as something driving you, but rather as vitality and vigor. This state does not interfere with sleep, on the contrary, you can be simultaneously aroused, excited and relaxed, able to choose more lovemaking, another activity or going to sleep.

Male Multiple Orgasms

"You never know a man until you know how he loves."
Sigmund Freud

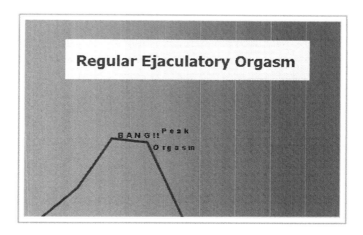

Stimulated by the hormone testosterone, men have been driven to populate the earth, planting their seed wherever they could at every opportunity. No small part of this drive is the intense sensation of pleasure derived from the simple act of ejaculating. Reaching a peak of sexual excitement, spewing ejaculate from the tip of their wand of light, and collapsing in a swoon of energy and tension release commonly takes only a matter of minutes for most men. As the simple diagram illustrates, this experience is a little bit like stepping off a precipice and flying into an abyss. The urge to do this repeatedly seems to be almost irresistible and becomes an obsession with many men. A typical male between the ages of fifteen and thirty can scarcely think of anything else day and night.

Alternatively, **Taoist and Tantric sacred sex practitioners** have perfected a mastery of this hot wild sexual energy. They have learned to ride the bronco and have tamed the stallion. These ancient practices originated in exotic locations such as Tibet, India, and China. For thousands of years they were kept secret for the benefit of a chosen few who learned to harness their sexual energy for health, longevity, creativity and ruling the world. Now these secrets are revealed in this manual of masculine sexual mastery, and are easily accessible to any male who wishes to rise above the common man with a bit of disciplined practice.

Sexual mastery requires **graduation from friction sex to high-energy sex**. High-energy sex involves learning to delay the involuntary ejaculation response. Lovemaking is extended over a period of hours (usually four hours or more) rather than recklessly spewing sperm in five to ten minutes of frantic thrusting more suitable to animals than gentlemen. While the common man seems to take some misguided satisfaction in being able to come as fast as possible—perhaps he is still worried about getting caught or that his partner will change her mind—the sexually charismatic alpha male will take delight in rising from one peak to another in a continuous ascent to higher and higher levels of ecstasy, satori and Samadhi.

As illustrated in the diagram below, at each peak of sexual arousal, the master will relax and rest, while performing simple breathing, muscle contraction exercises, and visualizations to circulate the hot sexual energy away from his genitals, moving it up through his entire body. Once the hot sexual energy has cooled down and become more manageable, active lovemaking can be resumed, building to yet another peak of heightened sensitivity and expanded consciousness. In this way the lovers can build sexual energy and excitement again and again to any number of orgasmic peaks. At some point counting the peaks and orgasms becomes irrelevant as you both enter into a continuous orgasmic intensely high-energy state.

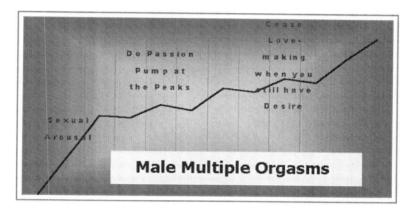

Paying Attention: What You Do Want

A core principle in masculine sexual mastery is to pay attention to what you do want rather than focusing on what you don't want. You must train your consciousness to focus on such things as pleasing your sexual partner, building high sexual charge, circulating hot sexual energy throughout your body and exchanging it with your lover, extending the physical pleasure, and expanding your consciousness. You do not want to focus your attention on avoiding ejaculation. Remember, you will always get more of what you pay attention to. When the focus of your attention is on "not ejaculating" you are really paying attention to what you don't want, and unfortunately, you are going to get more of it, not less. In other words, trying not to ejaculate is one of the quickest ways to ejaculate!

Trying to stop ejaculation is an example of the ordinary man's attempt to stay in control. But **the masculine sexual master understands that he controls nothing, nor does he care to.** Rather, he rises to the challenge of surrender, allowing himself to let go. In this way he will enter into the flow of the mystery. He will stay completely aware, witnessing each timeless moment as it unfolds. He has no goal orientation. He does not perform. He simply becomes the lovemaking. In this contemplative state of consciousness (where the lover and the act of love become one), the sexual master experiences complete freedom in a continuously flowing bliss state.

A sexual master is not a performance champion; rather, his lovemaking is an effortless artistic creation. However, much effort and practice have prepared him for this act of creation. It is to this effort and practice that we now turn our attention.

Awareness: Your Sexual Arousal

Prolonging lovemaking for hours is not difficult. There are a number of **simple techniques you can easily learn** to enable you to do this. A good starting place is to **map your sexual arousal process,** by creating a scale from one to ten so that you can always be aware of exactly how close you are to an involuntary ejaculation response. On your arousal map, one is the lowest level of sexual excitement and ten is the highest. While you are learning the skills of masculine sexual mastery you will try to stay below a certain level of arousal **where ejaculation becomes unpredictable**, but as your level of mastery unfolds, you will easily soar to the heights of bliss and ecstasy at the top of your scale.

Here is a description of what the various points on an arousal scale could look like. Of course, you will have to observe your own arousal process over many repetitions in order to complete your own map, but it may be helpful to have some ideas of what to look for. It really does not matter at all what anyone else's map includes at each point on the scale from one to ten; what you must do is become aware of your own.

Arousal Level One

Your penis is soft. Nevertheless, you find yourself thinking or fantasizing about sex. This is quite different from working on the next report for work. You may imagine yourself and/or your lover touching you sexually.

Arousal Level Two

Your penis starts to respond. Blood enters the penis faster than it is leaving and you show just the beginning of an erection. If you have pants on, you will feel your penis start to push against your pants. Your breathing may start to change, for example speeding up slightly or there may be some involuntary gasping for breath. You may find it difficult to focus your attention on some responsibility or task you have been performing. You may actively initiate sexual activity with your partner or engage in the beginning of self-pleasuring by removing clothing and/or touching yourself sexually.

Arousal Level Three

There is active sexual touching. You have enough of an erection (stage two or possibly stage three erection) for the beginning of intercourse. You do not feel any urgency to ejaculate, but your excitement is building rapidly including a strong desire to touch, fondle and please your lover. You also have a strong desire to insert your jade stalk into her fig pocket, which you may or may not have already done. Your breathing is faster and more irregular. You are feeling powerful. You may have an urge to make animal sounds, but this is easily manageable if you wish to remain quiet for any reason.

Arousal Level Four

You have a sense of overwhelming passion. You feel consumed by desire and an urge to lose control. You may find it difficult to avoid thrusting rapidly, even frantically to release the sexual tension with an orgasmic spasm. But you are still aware enough to make the decision to slow down and take more time. You are aware of where your partner is in her arousal and pleasure and know that if you ejaculate now it will disappoint her (and probably yourself as well). You choose to wait. You use intentional breathing—deep, slow breaths—to keep a lid on your rapidly building excitement. You may divert your attention to something other than the lovemaking in order to neutralize the urge to complete the ejaculation release (this is not necessarily a good idea, but is a common practice with many men). You apply some **PC squeezing** to help keep the urge to ejaculate manageable by circulating some of the hot sexual energy away from your prostate.

Arousal Level Five

Your breathing becomes more and more irregular, one moment you are panting, another moment you are holding your breath. Blood is moving rapidly through your body and your upper torso begins to flush, for example your chest, face, nose, or ears. You begin to tighten and tense various muscles in your body. For example you may squeeze your lover with your arms, clench your fists, close your eyes tightly, grit your teeth, arch your body, etc., in a way that is increasingly involuntary. You are becoming quite noisy in showing your excitement and appreciation. You may feel inspired and motivated to speak words of love and endearment in your partner's ears, amazing yourself and your lover with the poetic creativity not ordinarily available to you.

The urge to complete the orgasm with an ejaculation is becoming very strong. You can't seem to focus on anything else but the intense pleasure that you experience when you come. The anticipation of this pleasure creates an urge to ejaculate that is hard to resist. Your erection is now at least stage three and quite possibly stage four. You may start to think and worry about premature ejaculation and the resulting disappointment to your lover and yourself if you come too quickly. This could start a whole train of thought that ironically leads to losing your erection without any ejaculation.

Number five on your arousal scale may be the point at which **ejaculation becomes unpredictable**. Unpredictable does not mean imminent. In other words, you may come in the blink of an eye, or you could last for another hour. The importance of reaching this point (wherever on your scale it is) is that **you must make a decision to change what you are doing** in your lovemaking in order to allow the hot sexual energy to subside. For many men this is the first peak of arousal where they must slow down, relax, possibly stop and rest, focus on breathing slowly, doing PC squeezes, using visualization techniques, pleasing your partner, etc., to get the attention off the urge to ejaculate.

For those men facing a more serious problem of premature ejaculation, this critical point could actually be reached at level two or three on their arousal scale, or in extreme situations even at level one, where ejaculation is almost instantaneous with the beginning of sexual activity. But most men reach the point where ejaculation becomes unpredictable at five, six, or seven on their scale. With sexual mastery, ejaculation will not be unpredictable even at ten on the arousal scale, but this is a very high level of masculine sexual mastery and may not be attained until many years of practice.

Arousal Level Six

Getting to level six on your arousal scale without an involuntary ejaculation is a sign of developing ejaculation mastery, but happily there is still a long way to go. The degrees of physical pleasure, and the vastness of expanded consciousness available at the higher numbers on your scale are wondrous indeed and worth every possible disciplined effort to attain. To successfully move into level six and beyond requires the ability to be aware as soon as you go into stage four erection, to change what you are doing to quickly drop back to stage three, or to lose the erection completely, allowing the hot sexual energy to subside, and then returning to active lovemaking, building to another peak of sexual arousal. Getting to level six, means that you are able to ride a peak of arousal without going over the edge into an ejaculation release. You are able to move the hot sexual energy away from your prostate using PC squeezing, almost as fast as it builds, so the urgency to ejaculate involuntarily is significantly delayed. Your breathing is slow, deep and rhythmical.

Arousal Level Seven

At level seven on your arousal scale, you may experience an orgasm without ejaculating. Usually this will happen if the lovemaking has been extended over a period of three, four or more hours. This may happen in less time as your mastery grows (eventually within minutes), but often for months of practice it may take four hours or more of continuously building and circulating your hot sexual energy to gain enough energy charge to access this type of orgasm.

You have already reached a number of sexual arousal peaks, but have repeatedly backed off from the urge to take a release of the energy that has been building relentlessly. With this level of mastery you may have already navigated through four, five or six sexual peaks and have had perhaps one non-ejaculation orgasm. This orgasm lasted a minute or more, with energy blasting its way through the upper torso of your body in electric shock waves of pleasure and delight. Afterwards, you become relaxed, but not spent. There is no loss of energy, and no loss of libido. Your desire for further sexual activity is completely undiminished. You are ready and willing for more, as your lover is undoubtedly also. You have allowed your erection to subside, but can regain one without the slightest effort.

To play at levels seven and above on your arousal scale, you must be able to move out of stage four erection quickly. Your consciousness is so acute, that you are always aware of your stage of erection and can manage it voluntarily. You have already gained enough mastery to be able to maintain a stage four erection for a limited time, but are able to drop back as necessary. To do so you have become aware of the subtle internal signals that your body gives you of where you are on your arousal scale.

As sexual arousal builds, your prostate becomes engorged, enlarged, and bursting with hot sexual energy. At some point if this energy continues to build faster than you are able to move it away, like a pressure cooker, there will be an explosion; in this case an ejaculation. Certainly you may wish to have a voluntary ejaculation at this point and it will be a big one, well worth the wait. However, taking the ejaculation at this point closes off the possibility of moving into the superb levels eight through ten.

Your prostate will give you a preliminary surge of the familiar orgasmic pleasure that accompanies an ejaculation. This sensation feels exactly like the onset of ejaculation. But there is momentary separation in time between the orgasm and the start of the ejaculation. When you feel the beginning of this orgasmic sensation, the prostate has not gone into complete irreversible spasm. You have enough time to change what you are doing and this will short circuit the ejaculation response. To the extent that you have learned how to stay completely relaxed (instead of the usual tightening of your entire body) and the hot energy is moving up and away from the prostate, you may experience one or even a series of orgasms with no ejaculation.

Arousal Level Eight

At level eight you are regularly having orgasms, none of which includes an ejaculation. You are a now a multi-orgasmic man. There is no overwhelming urge to ejaculate, because the hot sexual energy is being circulated throughout your body. Nevertheless, this is a very challenging choice point for you. There is a tendency to become greedy with lust, desire and the saturation of physical pleasure available at this level of mastery. You can stay in stage four erection for long periods of time, for example with your lover riding on top of you wildly, but your are already at an edge of excitement that could spill over into ejaculation within the tiniest fraction of a single breath. Indeed, you may be experiencing a dull, aching throbbing sensation in the prostate area because so much hot sexual energy has accumulated over a period of hours of active lovemaking, and you simply can't move it away quickly enough. Many men allow themselves to come at this point to relieve the prostate discomfort, but this is a **voluntary ejaculation**.

Of course the alternative is to switch to a quieter mode of lovemaking, one that emphasizes the circulation and exchange of hot sexual energy, rather than the experience of more physical pleasure. You do this by becoming quiet and still, while maintaining full penetration. If you choose to shift your focus away from further physical pleasure to an expansion of consciousness, to a profound spiritual connection with your lover, you may experience the sexual/spiritual ecstasy of "whose orgasm is it anyway?" In other words, the boundary between you and your lover can completely dissolve; so that your experience is that there are no longer two of you, but only one.

"One and one makes two—these two are one." Al Link

Arousal Level Nine

At level nine, you go into the mystery and can experience extraordinarily profound altered states of consciousness. These mystical states can include out of body experiences, extra sensory perception, remote viewing, time travel, flashes and insights of the past (including past lives) or the future, communication with spirits, guides, and the dead, experience channeling or an in-pouring of creative genius or problem solving, etc. Nothing could adequately prepare you for the delightful surprises the mystery may offer to you if

your are completely surrendered, your heart is wide
open, your mind is clear of all thinking or judgment,
and you are completely free of egoism.

Arousal Level Ten

At level ten it is possible to have direct experience with
the divine, with God or Goddess. High levels of satori,
Samadhi, and enlightenment become available. You
may come face to face with your creator. You may
merge with the creator. You may become God or
Goddess with no separation remaining. This is home in
eternity—beyond time and space, without beginning or
end.

Navigating Your Sexual Arousal Map

Remember, ejaculation can take place at any level on
the scale and it is important that you know where on
your scale it becomes **unpredictable**. Wherever that
point is, represents a *choice* point for you, i.e., you can
choose to have an ejaculation if you want one, or you
can choose to change what you *are doing* to allow the
hot sexual energy to subside and become more
manageable, so you can later return to continue more
active lovemaking that would last several more *hours*.

How can you identify this 'point of no return' on your
arousal scale? Learning about your arousal cycle is a lot
like 'potty training'☺. Young children do not even
know that their bodies are giving them warning signals
that they need to pee, for example. Until they learn to

identify these signals and take the necessary action, they "get caught" which usually means peeing in their pants. The same thing happens with adult males who "get caught" by coming before they or their partners are ready. This may also literally be "in their pants" if the ejaculation is extremely premature.

Just as all children can learn to pay attention to the signals alerting them to the need to get to the bathroom, adult males can also pay attention and know when they are getting too close to ejaculation. With this conscious awareness, adult males always have the choice to have or delay the ejaculation. In this way **ejaculation becomes completely voluntary.**

What are the signals your body is giving you that ejaculation is very close? You will not know what to do to delay ejaculation unless you become aware of these signals. What are some of the signs your body uses to tell you how excited, turned on and close to ejaculation you are?

Body Signals for Voluntary Ejaculation

Four Stages of Erection

"I wonder why men can get serious at all. They have this delicate long thing hanging outside their bodies, which goes up and down by its own will... If I were a man I would always be laughing at myself." Yoko Ono

There are **four stages of erection**. For both you and your partner they are probably the most easily identifiable signs and the simplest to use for always being aware of your level of sexual arousal.

Stage one (lengthening and filling) erection looks like a normal soft penis. There is no externally observable evidence of sexual excitement or arousal, but we refer to this as a stage one erection because inside, you are certainly aware of sensation in your genitals. You start to think or fantasize about sex; you desire to touch yourself or your lover or to be touched by your lover. Intercourse is not possible in stage one, but you are probably thinking about and visualizing it.

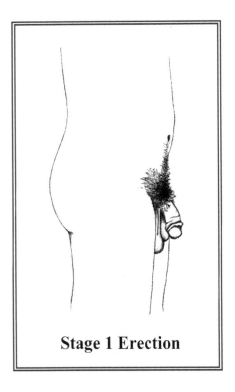

Stage 1 Erection

Stage two (swelling) erection is a partial erection. A stage two erection is starting to stand up but is not straight-up saluting. You can engage in intercourse with a stage two erection, but this requires a "soft entry". With a soft entry you or your partner manually insert the lingam (Tantric for penis) into the yoni (Tantric for vagina). First lubricate both the lingam and yoni with saliva, vaginal fluids, or a suitable lubricant (preferably a water-based or silicone lubricant).

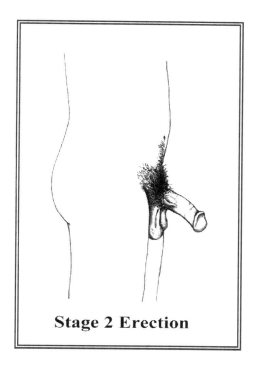

Stage 2 Erection

Stimulate a soft penis to a stage two erection using your hand to rub the penis against the vagina, or with fellatio, then use your hand to manually insert the penis. A stage two erection is sufficient for intercourse, but will not likely provide complete satisfaction for your partner.

Stage three (full erection) stands straight up and gives you a salute. Some men will ejaculate in stage three, but ejaculations are much more common in stage four. A stage three erection is quite adequate to give your partner completely satisfying lovemaking, but there is no denying the thrill for your partner of wildly riding a stage four erection. The major advantage of a stage three erection is that it allows the man to be fully engaged in active intercourse without concern about the overwhelming urge to ejaculate. Most men can learn to maintain a stage three erection while successfully delaying ejaculation for prolonged periods of time—for example, for hours rather than minutes.

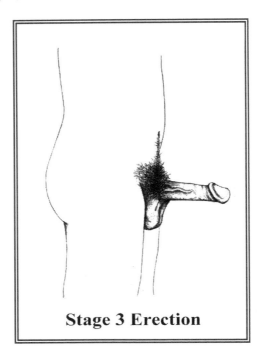

Stage 3 Erection

Stage four (rigid erection) is very proud and a sight to behold. Often referred to as a "boner," just the sight of one can bring some women to the point of climax. As Mark Twain said, "The penis mightier than the sword." Because the lingam is fully engorged with blood, a stage four erection is rock hard, noticeably harder than a stage three erection. It also feels very hot to the touch and may change color becoming brighter or darker. The danger is that for most men, **a stage four erection**

means that ejaculation is unpredictable, perhaps imminent. Sexual mastery requires that you must change or stop what you are doing and allow your erection to subside, which is a necessity if your intention is to prolong lovemaking over a period of hours.

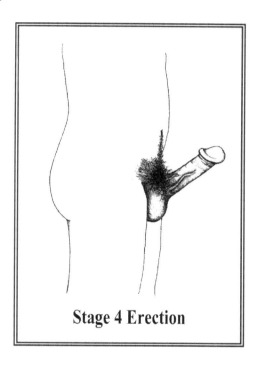

Stage 4 Erection

Erections Come and Erections Go

Ordinary sex is like a fireworks rocket. The ascent is rapid, followed by an intense explosion, and a cascade back to earth. A man can go through all four stages of erection in five or ten minutes (sometimes less!)

culminating in the spewing of sperm in an ejaculatory climax abruptly ending the lovemaking. This is really just screwing, not lovemaking at all, but based on this type of early experience (reinforced as the norm in Hollywood movies where an entire lovemaking scene can be filmed in under 60 seconds) men and their partners begin to believe that a man gets and keeps a single erection during every session of lovemaking. Obviously, if the entire lovemaking event takes less than thirty minutes from start to finish, getting and keeping a single erection the entire time is possible, and there would be no reason to question it at all.

On the other hand, a sexual master will normally extend lovemaking over a period of hours—four or more. It is not uncommon for Tantric and Taoist masters to make love for twelve hours or longer. It must be equally obvious that **no one would be capable, nor would they want to get and keep a single erection for hours at a time. With masculine sexual mastery there are periods of intercourse that start and stop throughout the lovemaking time; there is not continuous intercourse with active thrusting for hours on end**. This is one of the most common misconceptions about extended lovemaking practices. This misconception arises from the erroneous assumption that sex is intercourse, failing to take into consideration the countless other ways that lovers join in ecstatic sensual/sexual/spiritual union.

An **erection is a cardiovascular event**, which means that the lingam becomes hard when blood is trapped inside, and stays erect only as long as that blood remains. Blood is the carrier of oxygen and hormones to the tissues of the penis. In active lovemaking the oxygen is consumed and as the hormones are chemically transformed, waste products build up inside the penis and surrounding tissues. Unless the old blood is removed the man will become sexually exhausted and is in danger of ejaculating prematurely because of this fatigue.

In masculine sexual mastery, the man allows his erection to subside every thirty to forty-five minutes. As the erection subsides, depleted blood leaves the lingam, carrying with it all the waste products. With the resumption of active lovemaking after a period of rest, the man regains his erection as new blood enters the penis carrying with it a vital supply of oxygen and hormones. He is fresh, strong and virile again, able quite naturally to last long enough to match his female partner in sexual stamina without making a super-human effort.

Once you understand that it is neither desirable nor possible to maintain a single erection for hours at a time, you are psychologically prepared for allowing the erection to come and go, in fact for encouraging it to do so. You would not fall into the trap of worrying about why a man goes soft periodically during lovemaking. Rather, it is an important skill in masculine sexual mastery—that is to say, **the sexual master is skilled at managing his erection, knowing when to allow his penis to go soft and when to encourage another erection.**

This knowledge is an important key in avoiding the common problem of **performance anxiety**, which adversely affects so many male lovers. While it is true that men improperly sometimes treat women as sexual objects, women just as frequently treat men as success objects, with the close corollary that they also treat men as sexual performance machines.

Other Ejaculation Alert Signals

As you approach the point on your sexual arousal scale where ejaculation becomes unpredictable, your body may warn you with any or all of the following signals:

- Your *breathing* may become rapid, uneven, jagged or raspy.
- You may make *sounds* including animal growls, grunts and screams. Unless you are being intentionally quiet your natural tendency is to become noisy.
- Tightening, contracting, and tensing muscles is a clear sign of unpredictable ejaculation. *Tension* will be apparent in either your entire body or parts of it. You may clench your fists, squeeze your lover very tight, flex your stomach muscles and contract your buttocks.
- Due to increased blood circulation to the chest, neck, face, ears, and nose, *flushing* may occur in the upper torso.
- Your t*esticles* will pull up close to your body and your e*yes* will glaze over just before ejaculation.

Pre-Cum

Pre-cum is nature's lubricant, secreted by the lingam to lubricate the yoni during intercourse. A man can secrete pre-cum continuously over a period of hours from the end of his penis as long as he stays aroused to a stage three or stage four erection.

The popular silicone-based lubricants are copies of how pre-cum feels—very slippery. Urine has an unmistakable odor, while pre-cum is odorless. Semen is always cloudy whereas pre-cum is completely clear. If there is any cloudiness to this discharge you know that you are very close to a full ejaculation.

Internal Ejaculation Alert Signals

Internal body signals are the subtlest but also the most reliable indicators of how close you are to ejaculation. Once you become attuned to notice these signals you will always have a choice of whether to proceed in taking the ejaculation release or delaying it and going on to higher energy states. In other words, **at this point ejaculation will be almost completely voluntary**. Achieving such awareness requires that you observe your sexual arousal process through many repetitions. Fortunately this is an extremely pleasurable task!

The prostate gland is located below the bladder and surrounds the urethra as it leaves the bladder. The urethra is the tube through which urine and semen pass out of the body. The prostate secretes a thin milky fluid that lubricates the urethra and helps prevent infection. The prostate's primary function is to produce most of the fluids in semen, including the fluid that nourishes and transports sperm.

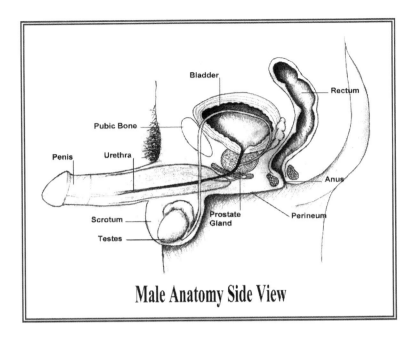

Male Anatomy Side View

When sexual arousal reaches a certain threshold of intensity, your **sympathetic nervous system** directs the reflex centers of the spinal cord to initiate the ejaculation response. **Usually this entire process is involuntary, but with the type of training offered in this manual you can make it voluntary.**

Internally throughout your genital area you have **smooth muscle tissue**. Another name for smooth muscle is **involuntary muscle**. What you will be doing with the exercises that we suggest in this manual is to **gain a degree of voluntary mastery over your involuntary smooth muscle.**

Once the ejaculation response has started there is no stopping it. Smooth muscles at the base of the penis contract every 0.8 seconds forcing approximately 5 ml of semen containing 300 million sperm out the tip of your lingam in as many as five powerful spurts.

During active lovemaking, hot sexual energy builds up to high intensity in the genital area with particular concentration in and around the prostate. The ejaculation response involves forceful contractions of the vas deferens (the tube that transports sperm from the testicles to the prostate), and contractions of the prostate, which adds prostatic fluid to the sperm, completing the mix that you know as semen.

Filling of the urethra activates internal smooth muscle tissues causing rhythmic contractions in surrounding organs including the erectile tissue of the penis. Simultaneously, most men (who have not learned to stay relaxed) contract the pelvic and abdominal muscles with powerful thrusting movements. The result is a tremendous increase of internal pressure, which forcefully expels the semen.

As the hot sexual energy builds with arousal, you will get to a point where it feels as if the orgasm is just starting to happen. This sensation is unmistakable—it feels exactly like the onset of ejaculation. If you have slowed down and are being very observant, you will definitely feel it. This sensation does give you enough warning to be able to change what you are doing and allow the energy to subside to a more manageable level. You can then resume lovemaking and build to another energy peak.

I've caught the signal, now what to do?

Mapping your arousal scale and becoming aware of the external and internal body signals warning you that ejaculation is close is not the most difficult challenge. Far more challenging is making the decision to delay the ejaculation. **The urge to ejaculate can be almost overwhelming.** However, knowing there is something better (high energy states of ecstasy and Samadhi for example) makes the job quite a bit easier. **The following techniques help you last.**

Stop

Stop—become completely still. Young men learn about this technique in high school, but perhaps you have forgotten this tried and true method for delaying ejaculation. Also, it is a critical point of timing to stop before the **autonomic nervous system** has started the ejaculation response. If the ejaculation response has already begun and you stop at that point, all that will happen is that you will experience a weak unsatisfying ejaculation.

After stopping you must also wait long enough for your sexual excitement and the hot sexual energy to settle down. If you resume active lovemaking too quickly, you will not successfully delay the involuntary ejaculation.

If you are particularly susceptible to premature ejaculation, stopping alone may not be sufficient. In this case you must also interrupt intercourse by withdrawing the lingam from her delicious yoni, or interrupt fellatio and withdraw from your lover's mouth.

Breathing

Every spiritual practice, every martial art, and every high performance sport requires mastery of the breathing process. **There can be no mastery of the body without mastery of the breath**. The ordinary man pays little attention to his breathing, allowing it to proceed on autopilot. Contrary to this, **Taoist and Tantric practitioners breathe consciously with an intention to influence sexual performance.**

Slow, rhythmical, deep abdominal breathing makes it possible to delay an ejaculation indefinitely for hours of prolonged lovemaking, thus opening the door for male multiple orgasms. It brings many other benefits as well, including stopping your thought process so your mind can be at rest, grounding your sensory awareness in the now moment, boosting your immune system, and controlling tension, anxiety and pain.

Men love to be in control, to feel as if they can make things happen. Unfortunately this approach to accomplishing what you want is NOT helpful in learning how to become a multi-orgasmic man. **Control is the enemy of ecstasy!** Instead you must learn to surrender, go with the flow, and leap into the mystery. Conscious breathing (long, slow breaths) during which you make your exhalation twice as long as your inhalation can aid you in the challenge to let go of the need to be in control by bringing your attention fully into the present moment.

Deep Belly Breathing Practice

- Sit, or lie down, in a quiet place where you won't be disturbed for 10 minutes.
- Relax your body by briefly tightening and then releasing each of its parts.
- Begin with your feet—contract, hold, let go—then move to your calves, thighs, genitals, buttocks, belly, chest, back, hands, arms, neck, face and scalp.
- Now switch your attention to your breathing.

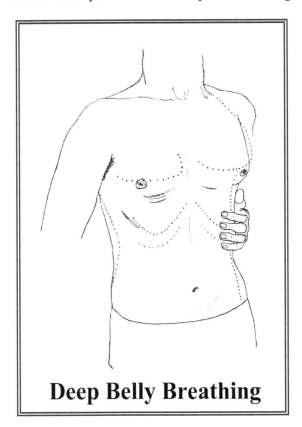

Deep Belly Breathing

I've caught the signal, now what to do?

- With your right hand on your abdomen, and your left hand along the bottom of your ribcage begin to inhale slowly through your nose.
- Push your belly out a little to help you pull the air deep into the bottom of your lungs.
- Push your ribcage out to fill the middle portion of your lungs.
- Slowly continue to inhale, filling the top part of your lungs until you are full of air—even in your throat and nose.
- When you are completely full, gently and without pause begin to exhale.
- Make your exhalation twice as long as your inhalation.
- As you inhale the life-giving air feel it bringing you vitality, focus and relaxation.
- As you exhale feel all tension, stress and negativity leaving with your breath.
- If your thoughts wander kindly bring them back to focus on your slow, deep inhale and exhale.

Lovers' Rhythmic Breathing

During lovemaking **harmonize your breathing with your partner, so that you breathe together in rhythmic unison**. Focusing on breathing together helps you tune in to each other, sharing an emotional and energetic connection. This is especially effective at the heights of passion when you want to draw your hot sexual energy up and away from your genitals.

Look into each other's eyes. As you slowly exhale, your lover inhales. As your lover exhales, you inhale—simple, but very powerful.

Sound

Sound carries energy. Every martial artist knows this. Perhaps you have observed that when a martial artist makes a hit, he makes a loud yell at the same time, because that yell carries the energy out of his body into the strike. **To successfully delay ejaculation, you must get the hot sexual energy up and away from the genitals** or there will certainly be an involuntary spasm of the prostate. **The more noise you make, the better.** Besides moving energy it gives your partner feedback about what you like and do not like and communicates your rising level of excitement.

Anytime during lovemaking, and certainly at a peak of sexual arousal make lots of noise—any kind of noise, it really does not matter. For example, as the lovemaking progresses sigh and moan to show your appreciation and mounting pleasure. Whisper and talk into your lover's ears saying how much you want, need, love and adore her. Talk wildly and lewdly when the level of excitement and passion builds to the right fever pitch. And at the very peak of excitement, where you want to level off and ride the wave of bliss, as you exhale send out a deep lion roar, allowing the sound to rise up from your genitals, from your scrotum. Feel the energy move up the center of your body as it is carried along by the yell. **Notice how the urgency to ejaculate is quickly relieved with this energy circulating practice**.

Testes Tug

A man's scrotum pulls up tight to his body just before ejaculation. When the testicles pull up in this way, there is very little reaction time before the ejaculation starts, so this is not a particularly helpful body signal alerting you to how close ejaculation is. However, knowing this, you can periodically gently pull the testicles away from the body, and this will help postpone the urge to ejaculate. You can do this yourself, but it is much more interesting to have your lover tug for you using her hand, or better still, her mouth.

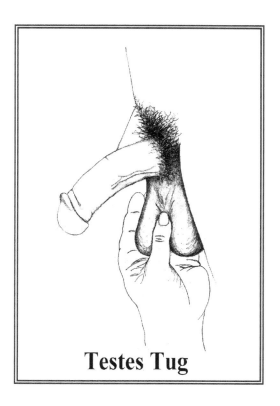

Testes Tug

Penis Tip Squeeze

This technique is very useful for delaying the ejaculation response during the self-pleasuring of masturbation, or when you are being pleasured manually or orally. It is not as useful during intercourse because of the need to grasp the penis with your hands.

The penis tip squeeze is perhaps most effective early in the learning curve of masculine sexual mastery. After you have gained some facility with moving the hot sexual energy up through your body with PC squeezes, breathing, visualization, etc., the penis tip squeeze may become irrelevant.

Split-second timing is critical in application of the penis tip squeeze when you are in a stage four erection. Assuming you have mapped your sexual arousal process and are aware of the ejaculation alert signals (external or internal) provided by your body, they will indicate when to apply the tip squeeze. The best signal for perfect timing is the internal sensation of the start of orgasm that you can feel in the prostate.

When you become aware of this signal, or any of the other ejaculation alert signals described above, firmly grasp the tip of the penis in one hand so that the palm of your hand closes over the tip of the penis. Do not try this if ejaculation has already started—it will hurt! Combine this squeeze with also applying pressure at the base of the penis where the shaft rises out of the pubic bone. One hand presses against the pubic bone, with the thumb on one side and the first two fingers on the other side of the shaft, while the other hand squeezes the tip of the penis.

I've caught the signal, now what to do?

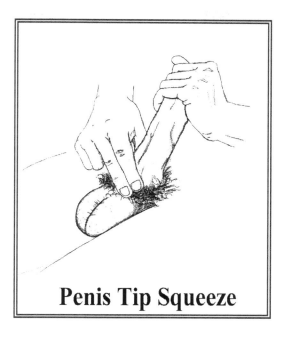

Penis Tip Squeeze

Wear a Condom

Condoms are essential for safer sex, but even if you know your partner is safe, condoms are effective in noticeably reducing the super-sensitivity of the glans (tip of the penis). This decrease in sensitivity does not diminish your pleasure but will almost certainly increase the amount of time during which you can engage in active intercourse without the urge to ejaculate overwhelming you. In fact, because you can last so much longer you and your partner will both get much more pleasure.

Have fun with condoms. Make putting the condom on a part of your love play. If you do not wish to use condoms, you might consider a topical application such as *China Brush* to desensitize the lingam.

Focus on Your Partner

"Men ought to be more conscious of their bodies as an object of delight." Germaine Greer

One of the most important lover's skills is the ability to remain completely immersed in the lovemaking, with 100% of your attention on what is happening in the moment. Paradoxically, you must get your attention away from ejaculation. **Many men use the simple technique of thinking about sports, cars, work, or some other topic. This is a common mistake, and one you are strongly advised to avoid**, because it takes you away from your partner, away from your connection, away from the moment.

Being fully present during lovemaking is essential if you are to reach the heights of bliss. **In ecstasy, the boundaries between the lovers disappear—it is as if you were one.** This is a state of profound mystical, emotional, and spiritual connection. If you divert your attention to something away from the lovemaking in order to avoid ejaculation, you are going to break the energetic connection with your lover and ecstasy will elude you.

One of the best ways to get your mind off ejaculation, but to remain completely immersed in the lovemaking is to **pay attention to pleasing your lover**. This is another example of paying attention to what you do want, rather than what you don't want.

I've caught the signal, now what to do?

**Few experiences compare to giving a woman
complete sexual satisfaction.** All great masculine
lovers take the most sublime pleasure in giving her
pleasure. Notice how she reacts when your tongue is
exploring around her clitoris, but also notice how her
clitoris feels on your tongue. Notice how she enjoys
when you suck on her nipples, but also notice how her
breasts feel pressed against your face. Notice how she
moans when you gently run your fingers up the inside
of her thighs, but also notice how her skin feels so soft
and warm against your fingers.

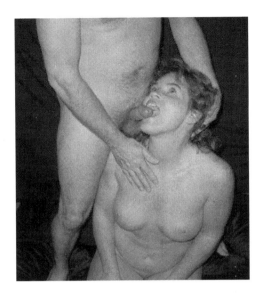

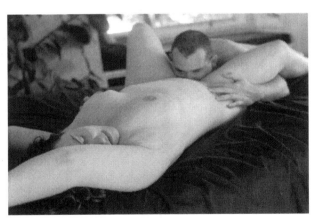

Slow Down and Foreplay

"A woman is ready 15 minutes after her man is finished!" Sad, but too often true. This is because **men are like fire** (they heat up and burn out quickly), while **women are like water** (they take a long time to come to a boil, but can roll along for quite some time once they get there).

I've caught the signal, now what to do?

Ordinary men are particularly challenged by this difference in the speed of arousal, but this is not a problem for the masculine sexual master.

One of the simplest ways to resolve this difference between men and women is to include lots of foreplay. The basic premise is this: **help her reach orgasm with your fingers, tongue, and lips before you start to have intercourse**. You may also consider using dildos, vibrators and massagers, to help create a better match between the warriors of love.

I've caught the signal, now what to do?

One of the reasons men seem to be in such a hurry is a basic gender difference, partly explainable by the hormone testosterone—men have a lot of it and women don't. But there are some conditioned cultural reasons as well. Because of the Madonna/Whore split so common throughout the world, and the sexual double standard that results from this misguided concept, young women are taught to say no, but men with hormones raging can scarcely think of anything else. When they find a girl who is even a little bit willing, they may rush to conclude the act as quickly as possible, because God forbid, she might change her mind! Or worse, her parents might arrive home early and there would be hell to pay.

Also, as young men explore their bodies with masturbation, they are shamed so badly by the repressive teachings from school, church and family that masturbation is bad, dirty and dangerous, they rush to come as quickly as possible so as not to get caught in the act!

I've caught the signal, now what to do?

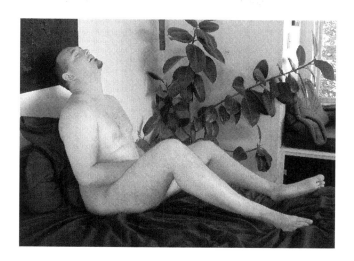

Now when you have the time and space for extended
lovemaking, good old John Thomas is still back in the
"I've gotta come now" days, and he's not going to slow
down just because you tell him to. That's like asking a
guy who's trained as a sprint champ to bring home a
gold in the 5000 meter instead. He may well be able to
make the shift but he's going to need some coaching.
You can train him with your mind, your muscles and
your breath or a combination of all three. It's not
entirely up to you either, your loving partner can assist,
after all it's for her benefit as well!

Opening Your Heart

Osho says about deep sexual communion: *"When in such embrace your senses are shaken as leaves, enter the shaking."*

Opening your heart has more than just an emotional significance. Energetically something important is happening as well. When you open your heart, energy moves freely in and out of that vital energy center—the heart chakra. When energy is free to move up away from the genitals through the higher chakra energy centers it is much easier for a man to delay his urge to ejaculate.

This may be a hard one to grasp, but **most women value the emotional, energetic and spiritual connection from lovemaking more than they value physical pleasure**. This does not mean that physical pleasure is not important to women, only that men can get preoccupied with their sexual performance, and they tie the self-judgment of their performance to the physical pleasure they can give their woman.

When men assume this goal orientation they often place an expectation upon themselves to achieve a standard of performance that can be totally unrealistic and which is almost certainly unnecessary, from the perspective of what the woman actually wants and needs. The resulting **self-imposed performance anxiety can speed the urge to ejaculate to the point where premature ejaculation becomes an issue**.

Possibly the single most important thing a man can do to delay ejaculation is to open his heart. This requires him to drop the need to perform as a sexual machine, to drop his sense that he is responsible for his lover's pleasure and sexual satisfaction, and to give up his desire to be in control. On the contrary, **what most women want is for their man to be emotionally vulnerable.**

Being emotionally vulnerable means simply sharing the truth of what is going on for you, including the feelings you are having about things. In particular, sharing those feelings like fear, insecurity and hurt, will help you connect with your woman in ways that can be more important than any amount of physical sexual pleasure. You will be amazed at how long you can last in lovemaking when you have opened your heart in this simple way and have dropped the need to perform.

Long and Short Thrusting

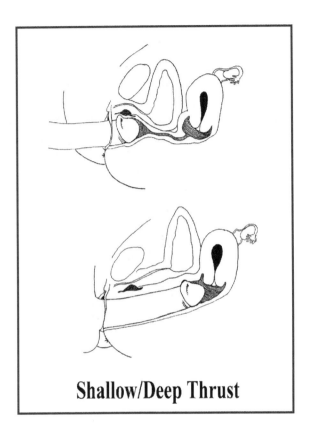

Shallow/Deep Thrust

How you thrust will definitely affect your ability to last during intercourse without an involuntary ejaculation. The long thrust completely buries the lingam as deep into the yoni as it will reach. The short teases the yoni with a partial penetration of perhaps one or two inches. By varying the strokes between deep and shallow you can manage your urge to ejaculate.

Because the full penis is enveloped and because the vagina is tighter the deeper you penetrate, long deep thrusts are highly exciting, intensifying the urge to ejaculate rapidly. The short shallow thrust builds excitement much more slowly, or helps you stay at a plateau of pleasure without going over the edge into an ejaculation release.

The **Taoist masters recommend alternating between a series of nine shallow to one deep thrust.** Experiment with the speed of thrusting, sometimes going very slowly, while at other times speeding up. For example try fairly rapid shallow thrusts followed by a long, slow deep one, then become completely still for a moment or longer to observe what is happening with your sexual arousal and energy. In this way you should be able to manage your building hot sexual energy quite effectively to delay ejaculation and extend the lovemaking.

Shallow
Thrust

Sexual Energy Squeeze

Progress in your ability to delay ejaculation and extend the lovemaking over a period of hours is primarily dependent upon your ability to circulate the hot sexual energy away from your prostate. The single most important exercise for doing this is what we call the **PC Pump or the sexual energy squeeze**. PC is short for **pubococcygeous**, a group of muscles surrounding your genitals and anus.

Variations of this exercise have been practiced for thousands of years in India and China, but have only recently gained recognition in the West. Dr. Arnold Kegel introduced them in the USA about sixty years ago (the early 1950s). He prescribed these exercises to women as a way to prevent and heal urinary stress incontinence. Since then, many women as well as many men have discovered the benefits of regularly practicing the PC Pump, now commonly referred to as **Kegel exercises**.

PC Pumping, or tightening and relaxing the muscles of your pelvic floor, offers men a number of interesting benefits.

1. Acts as a lock to prevent sexual energy from leaking out.
2. Acts as a pump to move and circulate hot sexual energy through your body, or exchange it with your lover.
3. Strengthens and tones the muscles of the uro-genital tract.
4. Increases your ability to get and maintain a hard erection.
5. Reverses and prevents premature ejaculation.

6. Massages your prostate gland for optimal sexual health. May prevent or eliminate the prostate enlargement known as benign prostatic hyperplasia, or BPH.
7. Extends and intensifies your sexual pleasure.

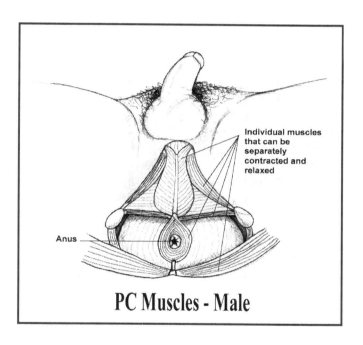

PC Muscles - Male

PC Pumping is so easy to do, one wonders why everyone does not already do it regularly as part of their daily (sexual) fitness regimen. It requires no equipment and you do not have to find new time out of your already busy schedule. You can do PC squeezes any time of the day or night, wherever you are, for example while standing in line at a bank or grocery checkout, while waiting in the doctor's office, or sitting at your computer.

53

There are a number of variations of the PC Pump, but the basic technique is to squeeze the muscles in the genital area, hold, and then relax. The squeeze we are referring to is what you do if you want to stop the flow of urine in mid-stream. That is exactly the right squeeze. The hold is what you do when you need to have a bowel movement, but have to wait because you are not near a bathroom. That is exactly the right hold.

Variations of the PC Pump include options for how hard you squeeze, how long you hold, and how rapidly you cycle between squeezes. You can also give a push out instead of just relaxing after the squeeze. The "push out" we are referring to is how you would push to start urination or a bowel movement. You can also experiment with different breathing patterns while you are squeezing, for example, hold your breath at the same time you hold the squeeze, or continue to breathe normally throughout the entire squeezing/relax sequence.

Over a period of two to three weeks we recommend that you work up to doing **100-200 PC squeezes per day** to **maintain optimal physical sexual fitness** regardless of your chronological age. This is easy to do by simply remembering to do a few squeezes, one or two minutes at a time when you would otherwise be waiting or bored.

The pubococcygeous muscle is actually a whole group of muscles. So when we suggest you squeeze the PC muscle, it is an important question: "Which muscle?" When you first start to practice PC squeezes, you will most likely tighten many muscle groups throughout your body, for example your stomach muscles, your buttocks, and you may even clench your jaw or fists.

I've caught the signal, now what to do?

This is a normal part of the learning curve for this exercise, but with many repetitions you will become proficient at tightening only **one muscle at a time**, **while keeping the rest of your body completely relaxed**. The ability to do this (selectively tighten one individual muscle at a time) is **a core competency for the masculine sexual master.**

After several weeks of PC Pump practice, you can start to focus on the challenge of identifying the individual muscles in the genital area and squeezing them one at a time. The critical muscles are these: perineum, scrotum sac, penis, buttocks (left and right buns), and anus. With some degree of mastery you can eventually put on quite a show for your lover by bobbing your penis up and down, or pulling your testicles up tight to your body and then letting them drop back down, squeezing the right or the left buttock, tightening the anus, or pulling up on the perineum, but doing only one at a time with all the others completely relaxed!

Here are some PC Pump variations to try.

The Beginner

1. While slowly inhaling, gently contract the muscles in your genitals.
2. During a slow count of 10, hold your breath as you keep your genital muscles tight.
3. Endeavor to keep the rest of your body relaxed— check your shoulders and your stomach muscles especially.
4. Exhale slowly through your nose as you relax your genital muscles.
5. Do this ten times.

Phase 2

This sexual energy squeeze adds another step.
1. Contract your PC muscles as you slowly inhale through your nose—five count.
2. For a count of five hold your breath and keep your genital muscles contracted.
3. Check the rest of your body for tension.
4. Now as you begin to slowly exhale through your mouth gently push out with your muscles—8 count.
5. Do this 10 times.

Phase 3

This requires more concentration and muscle control.
1. While inhaling slowly (5 count) gradually tighten your PC muscles.
2. Hold your breath as you quickly release and contract your PC muscles five times.
3. Endeavor to keep the rest of your body relaxed.
4. Slowly exhale and let your genital muscles go.
5. Do this 10 times.

The Master Squeeze

This version helps you gain more control over individual muscles. Try it after you've been doing the Beginner and Phase 2 and 3 for a week or two.

As you slowly inhale:
1. Tighten your anus.
2. Pull up on your perineum.
3. Pull your scrotum up close to your body.
4. Elevate your penis.

As you slowly exhale:
1. Let your penis go.
2. Release your scrotum.
3. Relax your perineum.
4. Relax your anus.

Repeat ten times.

If you do only one exercise from this manual, the sexual energy squeeze should be it. Begin with ten sets of each of the exercises listed above, then over a few weeks work up to several hundred repetitions per day. **The difference this one exercise can make in the quality of your lovemaking experience can be rapid and dramatic.** Do yourself and your lover a favor; start squeezing today!

At some point in your practice, you will probably find that the hot sexual energy moves in response to your thought and visualization alone, without any physical squeezing. Once you have attained this level of mastery, it is actually possible to have orgasms just by making eye contact with your lover from across a crowded room! This could take months to achieve or even years. When you are able to circulate your sexual energy with your mind alone, you may be tempted to drop the physical squeezing exercises. However we strongly advise that you **include regular PC squeezing into your fitness regimen for the rest of your life to maintain peak sexual fitness, i.e., strength and toning of the genital muscles**. Even though you can eventually move the sexual energy without squeezing, you cannot maintain the physical fitness benefits of PC squeezing without actually pumping.

The Passion Pump

The "Passion Pump", based on the Taoist practices of Master Mantak Chia, is one of the simplest and most effective methods of circulating sexual energy both within your own body and then to your partner and on to the cosmos. Practice it regularly in an unaroused state until you have all the pieces of this exercise flowing together in a smooth rhythm. Then add it to your masturbation practice for ejaculation mastery or use it when you are the passive, receptive partner—see "ways to love your man" p 116. Finally, when you're fairly comfortable with this practice at high points of arousal, add it to your active lovemaking, for instance during intercourse. There is a very noticeable difference practicing the Passion Pump in an unaroused state and when you are in the throes of sexual passion.

There are a number of sections to this exercise: controlled breath, PC squeezes, head actions and visualization which move your sexual energy in an orbit from your genitals up your back and down your front. It may take a while to have them all working seamlessly together so don't be discouraged. Simply by doing the exercise you are helping your energy to flow in a more fluid circuit, whether you "feel" it move or not.

Step One: Breath

1. Sitting comfortably, feet flat on the floor, begin to breath slowly through your nose
2. Count slowly to five as you inhale, filling your entire lungs—see Deep Belly Breathing p 36
3. Hold your breath for the same slow five count

4. Exhale through your nose, to the count of five
5. Repeat three more times and continue to breathe in this rhythm throughout your practice

Step Two: PC Pumping

1. During your fifth inhalation squeeze your PC muscles—it can help if you picture sucking air in through your genitals like you would with a straw as you inhale and squeeze—see Sexual Energy Squeeze p 52
2. Keep your PC muscles contracted as you hold your breath
3. As you exhale, slowly relax your muscles
4. Repeat three more times.

Step Three: Cranial Pumping

1. On the ninth inhale squeeze your PC muscles, then as you hold your breath, touch your teeth lightly together, and gently push your jaw straight back.
2. You will feel a very slight pull in the back of your neck.
3. Gently roll your eyes up to look toward the top of your head. This subtle cranial pump helps bring energy up to your crown chakra.
4. Finally, touch the tip of your tongue to the roof of your mouth—your tongue in this position completes the energy circuit, joining back and front meridians.
5. Leave your tongue touching the roof of your mouth throughout the rest of the practice.
6. As you exhale, relax your jaw and teeth, roll your eyes down and release your PC muscles.
7. Repeat three more times.

8. At first it won't be easy, but try to keep the rest of your body relaxed as you contract these particular muscles.

Step Four: Energy Circulation

1. On the thirteenth inhale, as you squeeze your PC muscles, visualize pushing a bright beam of energy up your spine from your genitals.
2. As you push your jaw back and roll your eyes up the energy beam is pulled up to your crown chakra.
3. As you slowly exhale, rolling your eyes down and relaxing your muscles, the energy spills over and flows down your front channel—through your third eye, your tongue, your throat chakra, heart, solar plexus and belly, back to your genitals.
4. Some people find visualizing a water wheel continually turning, pulling water up and spilling it over helps to bring their energy up to the head and then direct it easily down the front pathway.

Repeat this sequence for ten to fifteen minutes:
1. Inhale
2. Contract PC muscles
3. Direct energy up your back
4. Hold breath
5. Jaw moves back
6. Eyes roll up
7. Pull energy to top of your head
8. Exhale
9. Eyes look down
10. Tongue remains touching the roof of your mouth.
11. Relax PC muscles
12. Energy flows down to genitals.

13. On your last round, as your energy is flowing down your front channel, bring it to rest in your belly chakra—your hara, your sexual center—instead of having the energy continue on to your genitals.
14. Stay still and calm for several minutes and pay attention to what is happening inside.

Hara Center

Your belly chakra or *hara* (two finger widths below the navel) is the seat of your sexual energy. It is safe to store your energy there for use in other purposes later. For instance you can use this powerful energy for making decisions, creative activities, healing and so on. To access it simply put your attention into your belly chakra and direct the energy to wherever you want it: your head for clear thinking, your hands for painting, writing etc., your sore knee or back for relief. You may find it easier to send the energy if you drop it down from your belly chakra to your genitals then do a PC squeeze to help send it on its way.

Grounding Exercise

Grounding is a very effective process for calming and stabilizing. Grounding connects you with the earth, carrying overpowering negative energies down and away, much like a lightning rod. There are many methods for grounding. Try this one daily, as often as you think of it. Even if you don't "feel" anything while you are doing it notice the difference grounding makes to your overall sense of well-being. Grounding is also an excellent practice whenever you are feeling sexually "wound-up":

1. Sitting or standing, with your body relaxed, take a slow breath in through your nose.
2. Gently exhale through your mouth.
3. Focus your attention on the top of your head (your crown chakra).
4. Picture a funnel on the top of your head through which vital energy from the cosmos flows into your body—this is powerful, masculine, active energy.
5. As this sun and sky energy travels down through your body it gives you strength and vitality.
6. As it passes it also gathers up any negative energies you may be feeling—anger, lethargy, hyperactivity, grief, anxiety, fear.
7. Now focus your attention on your genitals (your root chakra) and picture a funnel there—with the small end of the funnel inside your body and the mouth of the funnel pointing down to the earth.
8. Allow the energy to flow through your lower funnel, away and down into the center of Mother Earth, taking with it all your tension; leaving vigor and calm in its wake.
9. Continue to visualize energy flowing in through your head, down through your body and out into the earth—bringing vitality and serenity and taking away stress.
10. Do this for a minimum of 3 minutes at a time.

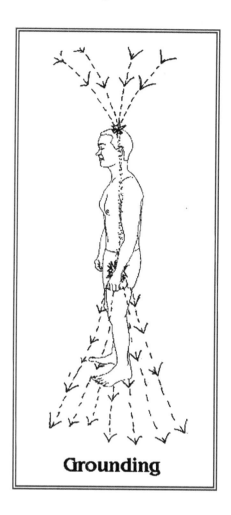

Grounding

Affirmations

Some men find affirmations to be a powerful way for the conscious mind to communicate what it wants from the subconscious. **The trick with affirmations is to stick to the truth and avoid lying to yourself.** Use affirmations before, during or after lovemaking to help develop your staying power.

An ineffective use of affirmations is to tell yourself you can already do what you cannot do. For example, to say to yourself, "I can last without ejaculating during hours of active lovemaking", when in fact you ejaculate within minutes after penetration would be lying to yourself. Using affirmations in this way actually retards your progress.

The effective way to use affirmations is to phrase them in such a way as to confirm that you will be able to do the thing you desire. For example, "I will quickly master building high sexual charge and circulating that energy through my entire body." Such an affirmation becomes a powerful vision of what you want to create. Once communicated to your deep subconscious, it can go to work to help you bring your affirmation into reality.

Smooth Muscle Biofeedback with Arginine

As your masculine sexual mastery training progresses your awareness will increase of what is happening within your body, in particular what your smooth (involuntary) muscles in and around the penis, scrotum and anus are doing and when (the timing of all this is critically important) they are doing it.

Using the methods explained in this manual it is possible for any ordinary healthy male to gain considerable voluntary control over many of his internal smooth muscles, particularly the ones related to sexual performance. In this way mastery in delaying the ejaculation response and extending lovemaking over a period of hours can be realized.

Powerful smooth muscle contractions expel semen from the penis in the ejaculation response. The prostate contracts 1-2 seconds before ejaculation and expels the seminal fluid into the urethra and out the end of the lingam.

It can be very helpful when you are first learning about your ejaculation response and trying to become more consciously aware of what your smooth muscles are doing to **set up an internal feedback through the temporary use of the amino acid Arginine**. This does not replace the need to use the techniques we have already discussed for building strength, stamina and focus, for example, PC Pumping, Passion Pumping, Grounding, breathing, etc.

Nitric oxide (NO) is necessary for erections to occur. With sexual stimulation your body naturally releases NO. This causes smooth muscle relaxation in the genital area allowing blood to flow into the penis resulting in an erection. The supplement **Arginine** (available on the Internet and over the counter at most health food stores in the USA) stimulates the release of NO.

You can gain the pro-sexual effects of smooth muscle relaxation and easily maintain a hard erection without the urge to ejaculate even with intense sexual stimulation by consuming 6-18 grams of arginine approximately thirty minutes before sexual intercourse or other sexual stimulation. Check a vitamin bottle in your cupboard to see the size of a 1000 mg. capsule. Six to eighteen grams of arginine in powder form would be from one to three heaping teaspoons. If you don't take enough there will not be any noticeable pro-sexual effect, but experiment to see how much is needed for you, as the quantity varies widely for different men.

In my (Al's) early experiments with arginine, six grams was enough and within thirty minutes I experienced a noticeable improvement in ability to maintain an erection during active sexual play with no urgency to ejaculate. This effect can last up to four hours or more. With a number of applications of arginine you will begin to become aware of how it feels when your smooth muscles stay relaxed. **The training effect is that you can begin to do yourself what the supplement helped you to become aware of and after that you will no longer need arginine.**

Caution: **Arginine is not suitable for everyone** or under certain conditions. Diabetics, borderline diabetics, cancer patients, persons with phenylketonuria (PKU), or persons who have had ocular or brain herpes should not use arginine. High dietary levels of arginine may cause reactivation of latent herpes viruses in a few susceptible individuals. If this occurs, discontinue use. **Consult your physician before using any supplements.**

Am I sure I want to do this?

Of course you are! Just remember that ejaculation and orgasm are not the same thing. **You are not going to give anything up.** You can have a voluntary ejaculation any time you want one. You can make love in whatever way you usually make love, anytime you want to. The practices of masculine sexual mastery do not deny you pleasure, on the contrary they offer the promise of a great deal more pleasure, and experiences that are much more than physical.

With the techniques of masculine sexual mastery you will learn to separate orgasm from ejaculation and in this way you can have any number of multiple orgasms in a single session of lovemaking. There is no shortage of pleasure for the sexual master! But in addition to physical pleasure, you will regularly connect with your lover in ways that are emotionally rich and spiritually profound. You can experience deep states of inner peace and tranquility as well as altered states of consciousness including bliss and ecstasy.

As for ejaculations, most men find that an ordinary ejaculation is rather a letdown (one of the most common ways men regularly deny themselves pleasure!) compared to riding repeated waves of sexual pleasure and bliss while having multiple orgasms. But don't be hard on yourself when you ejaculate involuntarily while you are learning. An **involuntary ejaculation is one way your body protects the health of your prostate until you learn how to successfully move the excess hot sexual energy away from the genitals during extended**

active lovemaking. At a more advanced level of masculine sexual mastery, you may find that ejaculation becomes quite irrelevant to your pleasure, while orgasm will be significantly enhanced.

By the way, **you can still have quickies**. We love short, intense snippets of lovemaking, but the major difference between what a quickie used to be and what it is now, is that our quickies do not end with Al ejaculating. Rather, they are brief interludes of teasing and enticement. These delightful, often raunchy encounters provide excellent stimulation and preparation for our extended lovemaking sessions—not a substitute for them. If short five to fifteen minute lovemaking sessions are the norm for you then you have much to look forward to as you progress with your practice of masculine sexual mastery.

Prostate Health

*"To succeed with the opposite sex, tell her you're impotent.
She can't wait to disprove it."* Cary Grant

**There is a common misconception within the
medical community that ejaculation is essential to
maintaining a healthy prostate**, in spite of the fact
that **the practice of delaying ejaculation dates back
thousands of years in India and China, with no ill
effects when practiced properly**. Naturally if a man
does not ejaculate and he does not move the hot sexual
energy away from the prostate he is going to get sore. If
he were to persist in such an unwise practice he could
cause harm to his prostate and possibly other organs in
the genital area. This is not what we are recommending
for you.

Delaying ejaculation during prolonged active
lovemaking is perfectly safe, assuming you are using
the techniques we have suggested to move the hot
sexual energy away from the genitals through the rest
of your body.

Your genital area is like a pressure cooker. As the
hot sexual energy builds with sexual stimulation, an
intense pressure accumulates and must be released. If
you have not learned how to circulate this energy
charge away from the prostate and you deny yourself
the release of ejaculation relying on sheer willpower
and physical strength, you are going to have problems.
But as long as you are able to move the energy away
from the genitals as fast as it builds, there will be no
discomfort at all. Indeed you will begin to experience
all of the benefits we have been alluding to in this
manual, for example sexual/spiritual ecstasy.

69

Until you have learned to successfully circulate your sexual energy, all you have to do is ejaculate to relieve any discomfort.

As you progress in your masculine sexual mastery practice you will first learn to delay the ejaculation response during a single session of lovemaking, thus extending that session for a period of hours. Eventually you can learn to end each session of lovemaking while you still have desire (without any ejaculation), so that **you can go days, weeks or even months at a time without ejaculating, but with a great deal of active lovemaking. The time between ejaculations will get longer and longer as your mastery grows**.

Remember, **you are not giving anything up** when you do this. On the contrary you will likely be regularly experiencing multiple orgasms without ejaculation.

How often should you ejaculate? Assuming you wish to move along rapidly in your learning, we suggest that you ejaculate as **infrequently as possible**.

Of course as you learn there will be many involuntary ejaculations, but **the only time we suggest that you ejaculate voluntarily is when you notice any discomfort in your prostate**—a dull aching, throbbing sensation, any other pain, or difficulty with urination. As soon as you begin to be sore in the prostate allow yourself to ejaculate and this normally eliminates any discomfort immediately, by simply letting off the accumulated pressure. **If any discomfort continues after two or three ejaculations you should consult your physician** to rule out any medical complications. For example you could have a urinary tract infection such as prostatitis, totally unrelated to your masculine sexual mastery practice. There are many over-the-counter nutritional formulas for urinary tract infections available at your local health food store.

The situation is simple and straightforward. **Any man practicing delaying ejaculation will almost certainly experience a sore prostate. What this means is that hot sexual energy is building in the prostate faster than you are able to move it away (the pressure cooker!). This discomfort should disappear immediately with one or several ejaculations.**

Don't try to be a tough guy by using your will power and physical strength to control ejaculations. Rather you must learn to coax and encourage the sexual energy to move using the disciplined techniques explained in this manual. Mastery is your key, not control, not will power, and not physical strength.

BPH

The condition referred to as BPH (benign prostatic hyperplasia or benign prostatic hypertrophy), reportedly affects more than 75% of all men over the age of 50, and large numbers of men younger than age 50. Few of these men are practicing the techniques of masculine sexual mastery, so this very common problem obviously has nothing to do with delaying ejaculation.

While BPH can be annoying and uncomfortable; it is not particularly dangerous and can be easily treated. BPH is essentially a swelling or enlargement of the prostate. A similar swelling or enlargement can happen to your prostate if you are delaying ejaculation and have not yet learned to move the hot sexual energy away from the genitals. So you will have similar symptoms, but the cause of these symptoms is not BPH. If you do have BPH you may exacerbate your symptoms with your masculine sexual mastery practices, and it would be a good idea to consult your physician for advice and treatment.

The **symptoms of BPH** include difficulties with urination such as:
1. the need to urinate quite frequently
2. having to get up in the middle of the night several times to urinate (but only urinating a small amount)
3. the urgency to urinate comes on rapidly and is felt very strongly (this is not the natural urge to urinate that any man will feel when his bladder is full)
4. or the feeling that you have not emptied out your bladder completely when you are done urinating.

These symptoms are the result of the fact that the prostate is wrapped around the urethra, so naturally any swelling of the prostate will restrict the flow of fluids through the urethra.

If your symptoms are caused by your effort to delay ejaculation you will almost certainly have the additional symptoms of **aching and soreness in the prostate, symptoms much less common in regular BPH**. This aching and soreness in the prostate is your best clue alerting you to the need to allow yourself to have an ejaculation to relieve the pressure that has been building up. Any discomfort and any interference with urination should subside within several hours after an ejaculation (or often immediately) if you don't really have BPH. If you think you might have BPH get it checked by your doctor, because an enlarged prostate can greatly diminish your libido and your capacity to engage in or enjoy sex—so take care of it.

Your doctor can advise you about prescription medications such as Hytrin and Finasteride for the treatment of prostate gland enlargement. These and other drugs act to relax the prostate and/or shrink the gland. If you do have BPH you might find that herbal nutritional supplements work as well or better and with fewer side effects compared with prescription drugs.

Doctors use two types of **medications to treat prostate gland enlargement.** Alpha blockers act to relax the muscles in and around the prostate. Alpha blockers include: terazosin (Hytrin), doxazosin (Cardura) and tamsulosin (Flomax). These drugs typically reverse prostate enlargement symptoms, particularly urination difficulties, within one or two days, but continuous use may be required to maintain the relief. **Side effects** include: headaches, dizziness, lightheadedness, tiredness, low blood pressure when standing, trouble with **erectile dysfunction (impotence), and abnormal ejaculation.**

A different class of drugs include Finasteride (Proscar and Propecia). Propecia is also FDA approved as a treatment for male pattern hair loss. Instead of relaxing your muscles, these drugs shrink your prostate gland, but usually take up to three months before you will notice a reversal of enlargement symptoms, and usually about one year for symptoms to be completely gone. **Side effects include: impotence, decreased libido and reduced semen release during ejaculation.**

Another relatively common condition is the inflammation/infection known as **prostatitis**. If you experience a discharge from your penis, burning during urination, or pain in the pelvis, groin or lower back, you may have some form of prostatitis and should **seek medical attention**, as this can be a very serious condition sometimes even requiring hospitalization. Frequently prostatitis is also accompanied by a fever. This condition is not related at all to your practice of delaying ejaculation. It is commonly treated with antibiotics. An alternative to antibiotics, with fewer side effects is cranberry extract.

Early in Al's practice of masculine sexual mastery he had some BPH-type prostate symptoms, although he was never diagnosed as having BPH. He relied on self-care rather than physician care and prescription drugs. With PC squeezing, perineum massages and nutritional supplements (a combination of those mentioned below), his prostate remains completely healthy more than two decades after all symptoms disappeared.

A far more serious condition is **prostate cancer,** a condition affecting perhaps 10% of men in North America. About 25% of the men who contract prostate cancer die from it, but many others live a relatively normal and symptom-free life without any treatment at all.

Sometimes the symptoms of BPH, prostatitis, prostate cancer, or just experiments with delaying ejaculation can be similar and confusing, even for trained medical practitioners. We recommend that you **consult with your physician** as you begin your practice of masculine sexual mastery. Have him examine your uro-genital and reproductive system to determine the status of your health. Be sure to inform him of your intended practices at delaying ejaculation and if any difficulties arise he will have some baseline information for comparison and should be able to quickly and effectively diagnose any occurring symptoms.

A **digital rectal prostate exam** involves the doctor feeling your prostate by inserting a gloved finger into the anus. A BPH enlarged prostate feels softer than a normal prostate, while a cancerous prostate feels harder, but this simple test is not adequate to diagnose prostate cancer, and may fail to diagnose BPH as well. Additional tests for prostate cancer include the **prostate-specific antigen (PSA) test** and a biopsy (testing a sample of tissue). The best test for BPH is a transrectal ultrasound. To identify prostatitis doctors typically test a urine sample.

The **PSA test** is a blood test that measures levels of the prostate-specific antigen, a protein produced in the prostate. The PSA blood test is becoming increasingly controversial because of so many false positive readings showing an elevated count. An elevated PSA count represents a warning signal to the possible presence of prostate cancer, for example, a normal value for PSA is less than 4 nanograms per milliliter, while over 10 nanograms strongly suggests the presence of prostate cancer. This test is subject to many errors of interpretation, for example BPH can also sometimes cause elevations of PSA even in the absence of prostate cancer. If the PSA is too high, almost certainly your physician will also perform the biopsy test for conclusive diagnosis.

Treatment modalities for these conditions are beyond the scope of this manual, but we recommend using some combination of herbal and other natural nutritional supplements as your first line of defense and only resorting to medical attention, drugs, or surgery if you do not get the results you want with the natural products.

Many health food stores carry **safe, natural herbal supplements to help maintain optimal prostate health. Beta Sitosterol, Saw Palmetto, Stinging Nettle, Lycopene, Zinc, Selenium, Vitamin E, and Essential Oils/Fatty Acids (fish oil) are some of the best supplements for this purpose.** Many nutritional companies offer excellent **prostate formulas** combining several or all of these ingredients in one capsule.

There are also a number of **pro-sexual formulas** to assist with your sexual performance, as opposed to prostate health. Many of these are quite effective in **helping men get and maintain erections, delay ejaculation and enhance physical pleasure**. We maintain a list of recommended nutritionals at our website. http://www.tantra-sex.com/aphrodisiac2b.html

Herbal, Mineral and Vitamin Supplements for Prostate Health

The four most important nutritional supplements for maintaining optimum prostate health are Saw Palmetto, Beta Sitosterol, Lycopene and Zinc. These can be taken separately or combined with other ingredients as they are commonly included in most prostate formulas.

Saw Palmetto

Saw Palmetto is the single most important nutrient to maintain a healthy prostate, with the possible exception of Beta-Sitosterol (see below). Saw palmetto berry extract is now used widely throughout the world for treatment of prostate problems. Also, because of its ability to block the formation of the hair follicle-killing dehydrotestosterone, saw palmetto berry extract enhances hair growth and luster, and helps regulate testosterone. It is also well known to rapidly alleviate symptomatic prostatic hypertrophy – and to reduce prostate specific antigen (PSA), a marker for prostate cancer. Saw Palmetto is a good source of fatty acids. Recommended dosage: 300 mg per day. Avoid if suffering from a disease of the gastrointestinal tract.

Beta Sitosterol

Beta-Sitosterol's effectiveness with regard to prostate health has been published in respected journals like the Lancet, Int'l Journal Immunopharmacol, Anticancer Research and others. This phytosterol produced by plants is known to be 3,000 times more powerful than saw palmetto berry extract. Recommended dosage: 100 mg 3 times per day with meals.

Lycopene

Lycopene is a powerful antioxidant found in tomatoes. It has been shown to be concentrated in the prostate and operates in synergy with Saw Palmetto to maintain a healthy prostate. Lycopene is a naturally-occurring carotenoid found in large concentrations in blood and body tissues. Lycopene plays an important role as a potent cancer preventive agent (especially of the lungs and prostate), a defender against UV skin damage, and as one the most important quenchers of singlet oxygen free radicals, making it a vital supplement to be taken daily. Lycopene packs an antioxidant punch at least two to three times more potent than beta carotene. Recommended dosage: 15 mg per day.

Zinc

Zinc is essential for a healthy prostate. Zinc Picolinate or Gluconate is available in capsules, powder or lozenges. Human and animal studies have demonstrated that zinc stimulates cell growth, enhances immunity, improves male sexual functions, helps skin structures and fights free radicals. Recommended dosage: 30 mg per day.

Stinging Nettle

Extracts of Stinging Nettle have been widely used in Europe for the treatment of Benign Prostatic Hypertrophy (BPH). With similar pharmacological actions to saw palmetto berry extract, Stinging Nettle has been extensively tested and found to be effective as a single nutrient or in combination with other botanical factors. Recommended dosage: 120 mg per day between meals.

Massage

Perineum Massage

The perineum is the area between your anus and scrotum. It is sometimes referred to as the "**million dollar spot**" or "**male p-spot**" (compared to the g-spot for women as a source of pleasure). **Men love it when their partner pleasures them with their hands or mouth by tapping, pressing, massaging, licking and sucking this highly sensitive erogenous zone.**

The perineum is also a key for any man learning to delay ejaculation because the prostate gland can be stimulated and massaged directly through the perineum. **Massaging the prostate through the perineum is one of the surest ways to move excess sexual energy away from the area.**

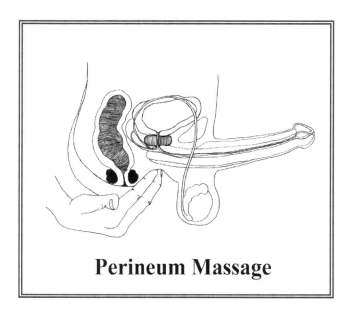

Perineum Massage

Apply your fingers as shown in the diagram. Press into the perineum, at about the halfway point—slightly closer to the anus than the scrotum—until you feel a firm lump (the prostate is about the size of a small walnut or a large grape). Rotate your fingers clockwise and counterclockwise alternately for two-three minutes. Experiment with various pressures and speed until you discover the right combination for best results. This will vary over time. An excellent variation is to fold a piece of silk over and massage the perineum through the silk which seems to have special energy dispersion properties, to say nothing of its sensual slippery softness. **We highly recommend a short prostate massage through the perineum after every session of lovemaking.**

Anal Massage

"The last sexual frontier isn't some intergalactic data fuck: it's your ass." Lisa Palac

As you can see from the diagram above, **the prostate can also be reached internally through the anus. Men can hold a great deal of tension in the genital area, and particularly around the anus.** Most heterosexual men are comfortable with the act of penetrating a woman during intercourse, but are much less comfortable (or possibly even terrified!) with the idea of being penetrated through the anus during lovemaking or as part of an energy circulating exercise. **For a male to allow himself to be entered through the anus requires serious surrender.** The lover being penetrated is in a most vulnerable position, and men are used to being in control. **Surrender is one of the core competencies of all forms of sacred sex practice.**

Exploring internal prostate massage through anal penetration is one of the quickest ways for men to learn surrender in the art of love. If your lover is skilled, an internal prostate massage is **also a source of extraordinary pleasure**. There are a number of excellent videos to help you learn how to give an anal prostate massage or anal pleasure massage. Any man who learns how to receive this pleasure will never again be referred to as "tight ass".

1. The man lies on his stomach with the option of placing a towel-covered pillow under his hips for a better angle of penetration.
2. Encourage relaxation by gently rocking his body back and forth and applying light massage to his shoulders, back, buttocks and thighs.
3. Wear latex gloves (use vinyl if there is any latex sensitivity or allergy). Use a generous amount of lubricant (silicone-based lubricants are recommended) and begin massaging the tissues around the anus with circular motions and gentle stretching.
4. Remember to breathe slowly and deeply.
5. Take as long as required to coax the anal muscles into complete relaxation.
6. Only proceed when the anal tissues open and invite you to come in. With your palm facing down toward the floor, insert an index finger, very slowly and very gently, into the anal canal.
7. Approximately one or two inches into the rectum, you will feel the prostate gland (a firm lump about the size of a small walnut or a large grape). Gently circle the prostate with your finger and experiment with pressing on it at various points with alternating

pressure and firmness according to your lover's reaction.

8. With your free hand continue massaging other parts of his body. Also, you can press the heel of your hand on his sacrum at the coccyx.

9. When you are ready to stop, remove your finger with tantalizing slowness.

10. Wash yourself and your lover thoroughly using soap and water.

Relaxing Full-Body Massage

A tense man is a man prone to premature ejaculation. One of the simplest and most effective ways to delay ejaculation is to **become completely relaxed throughout your body.** A **full-body massage** lasting as little as five to seven minutes, with particular emphasis on the large muscle groups in the shoulders, back, buttocks, and legs will rapidly release stress and tension from a man's body, while at the same time encouraging energy to move through the body smoothly. **This one technique can add hours to extended lovemaking**, because the urge to ejaculate will be significantly delayed. There are a number of excellent books and videos to learn the basics of erotic and relaxation massage.

Acupressure

Acupressure—applying firm, even pressure to specific points along your body's energy pathways—can greatly enhance your ability to delay ejaculation. Acupressure relaxes tissues, increases blood circulation, and allows energy to flow more smoothly. While there are more than 350 acu-points along your energy meridians we will only deal here with a few that are specifically relevant for male sexual pleasure, potency and stamina. For more extensive information on acupressure, particularly as it relates to sexual health and pleasure, refer to the work of Michael Reed Gach, especially his book *Acupressure for Lovers.*

You can press on the acu-points yourself or your partner can press them, either **before, during, or after lovemaking.** Use the tips of your fingers and push straight down on the spot, starting very lightly and gradually increasing the force. Maintain the pressure for at least one full minute—two or more is better—before slowly releasing. **Don't worry about getting exactly the right spot** at first—you'll feel it when you're there. It's more important to remember that **"slow" and "gradual" are essential concepts for your touch**.

Sea of Intimacy

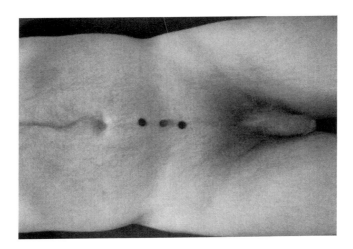

The "Sea of Intimacy" points are on your belly, extending in a straight line from about an inch and a half below your navel to just above your pubic bone.

Pressing these helps you in a number of ways:
1. during sex stomach muscles often tense up so your energy can't flow freely, pushing on these points relaxes the muscles
2. it improves your reproductive and urinary system functions
3. the Sea of Intimacy corresponds with your belly chakra, which is your sexual center, pushing on these points gives you more sexual pleasure
4. men who ejaculate prematurely can benefit immensely by pushing on these acupoints two times daily, and modifying their diet to include lots of fish and no sugar for 60 days or more.

Mansion Cottage and Rushing Door

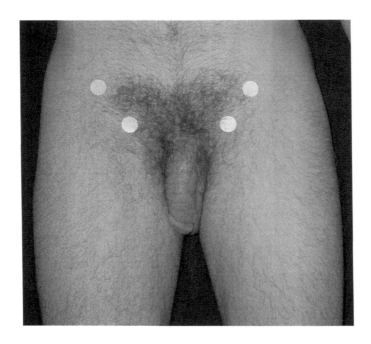

These spots are in your groin crease, where your legs meet your torso. You can find them in about the center of the crease on either side of the artery. Sexual frustration often gathers here, pressing on these spots releases that frustration and allows energy to flow feely to the genitals, greatly enhancing your sexual pleasure.

Inner Meeting

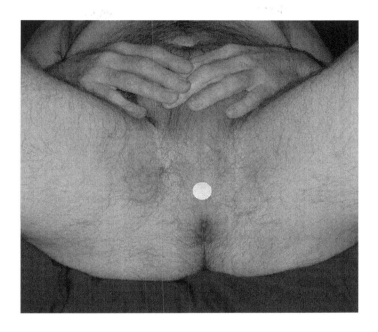

"Inner Meeting" is at the center of the perineum, the importance of which we've already stressed because of its relationship to the prostate gland. Pressing on this spot before and after lovemaking helps to move your sexual energy away from the prostate. You can also **press on it just as you are coming close to ejaculation**. If you get the right timing, pressure and location, you will block the flow of semen, channeling it through the prostate where it will be absorbed into the bloodstream. You may still ejaculate but the fluid will be mainly clear, with very little cloudiness from semen. Your orgasm will be intense but your energy depletion will be minimal. It may take some practice to hit this spot just so, but it can be very helpful as you are learning to move your sexual energy.

Sea of Vitality

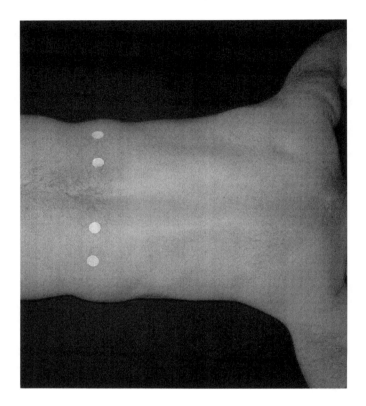

There are four "Sea of Vitality" acu-points, two on each side of your back approximately two and four finger widths out from the backbone on a line with your belly button. They enhance sexual vitality, strengthening your reproductive and adrenal systems. Press these points while you hug each other!

Sacrum

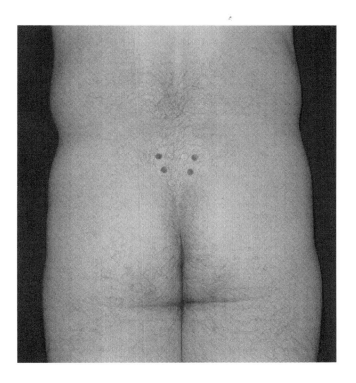

There are a series of acu-points grouped together in your sacrum, or "tailbone". You can feel them as slight indentations in the bone. Pressure on these points connects with the sacral nerve, sending very pleasurable sensations to your groin. Your partner can push these with fingertips or with the heel and palm of her hand. You can also press them yourself by lying on your back, hands beneath you, palms down, knuckles fitting into the acu-points. The weight of your body provides the pressure.

Bigger Stream

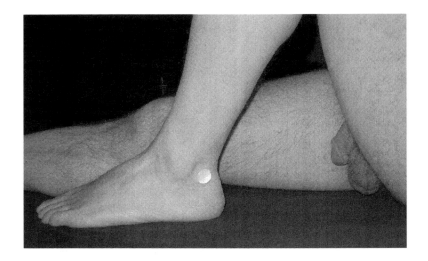

On the outside of your ankle, halfway between the
Achilles tendon and your ankle bone lies "Bigger
Stream", which benefits your sexual capacity and eases
sexual tension.

Pubic Bone & Collar Bone

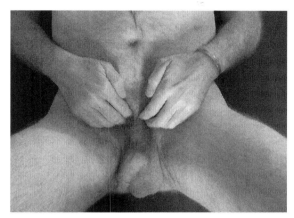

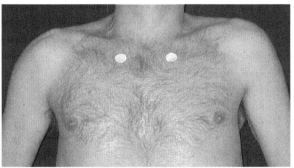

This brief acupressure routine practiced twice daily—
for instance when you wake in the morning and before
you go to sleep at night—will help you build your
capacity to delay ejaculation. As you lay on your back,
knees bent and feet flat on the bed, rub your pubic bone
firmly and quickly with your fingers for a minute and a
half. You are stimulating the "Crooked Bone" and
"Transverse Bone" points on your pubic bone. Then for
about one minute massage "Elegant Mansion"—the
indentations below the center of your collar bone—to
aid your entire sexual system's potency.

91

Aphrodisiacs: Increasing Sexual Desire and Capacity

Strengthen Erection, Delay Ejaculation, Increase Libido

Are you among the millions of people worldwide who are otherwise healthy but who've lost interest in sex? Do you find it boring and routine? Are you so tired that you'd rather nap than make love? Do you think TV is more stimulating than your partner? Do you have physical symptoms, like vaginal dryness or difficulty with erection, that make sex unpleasant?

As a relationship matures it is common, but definitely not necessary, for sex to become predictable and unexciting. One of the first places to start improving your sex life is to elevate your general mood and increase your energy level. This is good advice not only for improving sex but also for most other things in your life.

Herbal supplements are now entering mainstream medical practice, with one in three primary care doctors recommending them to patients at least weekly, most frequently for people with mood and emotional complaints. About as many doctors recommend herbal supplements for fatigue and lack of energy. Doctors also practice what they preach, with one in four doctors personally consuming herbal supplements.

So, let's assume you have covered the basics. You pay attention to what you eat and take some nutritional supplements. You follow a regular routine for physical

92

fitness. You are reasonably healthy. There are no organic health problems interfering with your sexual performance, or you have consulted a physician and they are being treated allopathically with drugs. (Note that many prescription drugs are known to interfere with sexual desire and performance. If you take any prescription medication, ask your doctor about such side effects. It may be possible to prescribe a different medication that won't interfere with your sex life.)

If you are not doing these things, you may consider changing your habits before you experiment with aphrodisiacs. Regular exercise, good diet and basic nutritional supplements may be all you need to revitalize you sex life.

Ideally we could also assume that you have set aside old beliefs and conditioning about your sexuality. You have moved beyond shame and guilt. You have had help in dealing with any sexual abuse or trauma. You understand and believe that sex is natural, good and wondrous. If you lack sexual skill and technique, and your imagination fails to motivate you to experiment by trying new things, perhaps a workshop or some private coaching is in order. Or read some good books on sexual technique.

Even if you have done all of these things, perhaps you are still looking for more and wonder if aphrodisiacs might be it. They are definitely worth experimenting with, but be warned, many of them may have side effects for some people. If you want to consume any item mentioned consult your physician first. If you do decide to use them, start out slowly and experiment carefully to see how each of them works for you. **Try them one at a time** to see what each one does on its own and how **your body** responds to its use before you consume several at the same time.

What are Aphrodisiacs?

An aphrodisiac is something that increases your libido. It turns you on and increases your **desire** to have sex, or it may reduce your usual inhibitions about sex. Aphrodisiacs may also improve your **ability** to have sex. This means that under the right circumstances, almost anything could have aphrodisiac qualities, but most people think of something to eat or drink when they think of aphrodisiacs.

Aphrodisiacs are never an alternative to healthy sexual attitude, doing your inner work to remove psychological barriers to sexual intimacy, or sexual skill mastery, but they can be lots of fun.

Aphrodisiacs may also be exactly what is needed when sexual dysfunction is caused by physiological/organic causes, e.g., peripheral vascular disease, hardening of the penile arteries, diabetes mellitus, prostate enlargement (BPH), high levels of pituitary gland hormone prolactin, low testosterone (hypogonadism}, and andropause (hormonal changes accompanying aging in men).

Selected Aphrodisiacs

Here is a brief summary of several aphrodisiacs that can enhance your sexual desire, help you experience more pleasure and perform better as a lover. We explain their general properties, how to use them, and where to get them.

Where possible use a product with **standardized extract**. This means that the product is guaranteed to contain a certain percentage of the active ingredient(s). Consult labels carefully to determine quantities of all ingredients. Follow dosage recommendations on the product label.

Some of the products described here are formulated to boost your libido, strengthen erection capacity, and increase sexual stamina. Some assist in boosting testosterone or maintaining testosterone/estrogen/ progesterone balance. Others are designed to improve your general well-being, increase your energy, and enhance your mood–all of which lead to better sex!

"The body is able to manufacture hormones, neurotransmitters, and neuropeptides only when fed certain essential ingredients. Many traditional aphrodisiacs are high in amino acids and the required vitamins and enzymes, which is why they really do work." Dr. Cynthia Mervis Watson, M.D.

Don't let the strange sounding names and exotic places they come from throw you off from considering the use of aphrodisiacs. These items are not any more unusual than many things now part of our regular vocabulary and consumption, for instance, aspirin.

Arginine

The **amino acid arginine** is an immune system enhancer and powerful growth hormone stimulant. It plays a role in many body tasks: wound healing, circulation and sexual function.

In response to sexual stimulation, your body releases **nitric oxide (NO)** in your genitals. This causes the smooth muscles to relax and blood flows into the penis resulting in erection. Both arginine and **ginkgo biloba** have both been shown to enhance NO levels in your body. In the absence of sufficient levels of NO sexual arousal and erection will not occur regardless of the amount of stimulation offered. "Arginine is absolutely necessary for the production of NO....Some scientists studying these phenomena have concluded that up to 90% of all impotency can be reversed by NO (and by implication, the use of arginine)."[i]

The erection promoting drug Viagra from Pfizer increases blood flow into the penis, or into the vaginal area for women, but this drug has many known side effects and there were 69 confirmed deaths attributed to Viagra use by the fall of 1998!

Amino acids are the building blocks of protein. If arginine is ingested with food, it will be digested as protein, and the pro-sexual benefit will be lost. Therefore arginine should be taken on an empty stomach, at least one hour before eating or two hours after eating. The best pro-sexual, erection enhancement, and sexual excitement stimulation, effects will be experienced if you ingest arginine approximately 30-60 minutes before sexual activity.

including "depression, fatigue, abdominal weight gain, alterations in mood and cognition, decreased libido, erectile dysfunction, prostate disease, and heart disease…"

Estrogen/Testosterone/ Progesterone Hormone Balance

"One report showed that estrogen levels of the average 54-year-old man are higher than those of the average 59-year-old woman." Too much estrogen and not enough testosterone is common with men over the age of 40, and very common with men over the age of 50, but the condition is normally easily treatable with over the counter herbal nutritional supplements.

Your body may actually produce lots of testosterone, but much of it gets converted to estrogen. You can also have lots of total testosterone, but not enough is freely available for sexual arousal and performance, resulting in erectile dysfunction and loss of libido.

A direct approach of administering testosterone may prove ineffective or even make the situation worse, if that testosterone is also transformed into estrogen. Men do need some estrogen, but too much is associated with a host of undesirable health risks, including various cancers, heart disease and prostate enlargement (BPH).

When there is too much estrogen present in a man's body, it will attach to testosterone receptor cells and block the testosterone from reaching the cells. The result is loss of sexual desire and difficulty with erections, among other things. "When an estrogen molecule occupies a testosterone receptor site on a cell membrane, it blocks the ability of serum testosterone to induce a healthy hormonal signal. It does not matter how much serum free testosterone is available if excess estrogen is competing for the same cellular receptor sites."

Ideally you would like to restore the estrogen/testosterone balance so that it is close to the benchmark for a healthy male of 21 years. Many medical doctors hesitate to suggest such a protocol, because of a fear that increasing testosterone may be associated with prostate cancer. But there is little evidence supporting this assumption. It is certainly true that testosterone should not be stimulated if a man already has prostate cancer, but there is no reason to suppose that testosterone boosting causes prostate cancer in an otherwise healthy male.

Some of the health benefits of testosterone include the following: protein synthesis for maintaining muscle mass and bone formation, improves oxygen uptake throughout the body, helps control blood sugar, regulates cholesterol, helps maintain immune surveillance, youthful cardiac output and neurological function, and is also a critical hormone in the maintenance of healthy bone density and red blood cell production.

The critical factor is how much free testosterone is available and whether that free testosterone can bind with testosterone receptor cells. Two common problems are: 1) not enough free testosterone and 2) testosterone receptor cells that are blocked because estrogen has

attached to them thus preventing access by the
testosterone molecules.

"Without adequate levels of free testosterone, the
quality of a man's sex life is adversely affected and the
genitals atrophy. When free testosterone is restored,
positive changes can be expected in the structure and
function of the sex organs."

There are 2.8 million cases of prostate disease reported
annually in the United States. Unfortunately in 2004
alone there were approximately 230,110 new cases of
prostate cancer, according to the American Cancer
Society. Prostate cancer is the second leading cause of
cancer deaths of men in the United States, after lung
cancer, and the sixth leading cause of death of men
overall over the age of 65. The reality is that few men
ever consider the walnut-sized fibrous gland located
just below the bladder, until it starts to give them
trouble. A survey reported in the London Times found
that 89 percent of the men surveyed did not know
where the prostate was located.

Whether or not the anatomical position may escape the
vast majority of men, the sobering fact is that after the
age of 50, the prostate begins to hypertrophy, or
increase in size. This enlargement of the prostate is
known as benign prostatic hyperplasia (BPH). Often
one of the initial annoyances of BPH arises from the
fact that the urethra (the tube that carries urine from the
bladder) runs through the middle of the prostate. This
swelling of the prostate usually manifests as urinary
problems: urinary frequency, urinary hesitation,
reduced urinary flow, etc.

High levels of testosterone are associated with superior cardiovascular health. Low levels of testosterone correlate with increased risk of developing coronary heart disease and other physiological manifestations of atherosclerosis. Boosting testosterone levels may prevent or even retard serious cardiovascular disease, while causing no serious side effects.

Other authorities agree. According to Lane Lenard, Ph.D., testosterone levels decline predictably as men age, as shown in the box below. According to Lenard, "the evidence so far collected suggests that low testosterone plays a causative role in virtually every factor identified to increase the risk of heart disease [and many other illnesses as well!]. Research also shows that restoring testosterone to levels that are normal for a 30-year-old can go a long way toward preventing or reversing these risk factors."[iii]

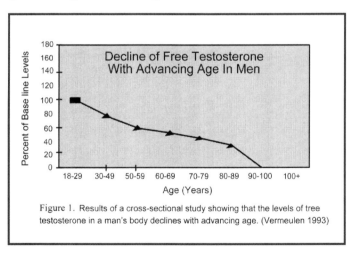

Figure 1. Results of a cross-sectional study showing that the levels of tree testosterone in a man's body declines with advancing age. (Vermeulen 1993)

Your level of testosterone can also dramatically affect your libido, your erection and your ejaculation. According to Jane Brody, "Testosterone is 'the hormone of desire,' the substance that acts on the brain to stimulate sexual interest, sensitivity to sexual stimulation and orgasmic ability in both sexes."[iv]

According to Dr. Lenard, trying to boost testosterone with anabolic steroids is very dangerous as these drugs are quite toxic, apparently causing serious problems with heart, liver and prostate, as well as mental disturbance and even impotence.

We do NOT recommend androstenedione supplements to boost testosterone. There is now some concern that the various andro supplements may actually cause an increase in estrogen, not testosterone. An enzyme called "aromatase," especially prevalent in fat cells, converts testosterone to estrogen. Since most men lose muscle and gain fat as they age, aromatase activity increases, reducing testosterone even as it increases estrogen.

Thus as men age, they may also experience elevated levels of estrogen as the balance between estrogen and testosterone shifts in favor of estrogen. This can lead to increased risks of heart disease, pancreatic cancer, and prostate cancer, as well as gynecomastia, the abnormal enlargement of breasts in men. Both men and women require the proper balance of testosterone and estrogen. Maintaining this balance becomes increasingly difficult with advancing age.

Three supplements are excellent for helping to maintain a healthy and youthful balance between testosterone, estrogen and progesterone. They are DIM/diindolylmethane, chrysin and Indole-3-Carbinol.

DIM

DIM, active ingredient diindolylmethane, is a phytonutrient found in broccoli, cauliflower, cabbage and brussel sprouts. DIM, unlike other phytonutrients, e.g., soy isoflavones, has no hormonal properties in itself. Studies show it works indirectly by increasing the activity of enzymes that control estrogen production. DIM boosts levels of good estrogens called 2-hydroxy estrogens and reduces levels of bad estrogens which are 16-hydroxy and 4-hydroxy estrones. Both forms of bad estrogen are carcinogens. There's evidence that benign prostate enlargement and some types of prostate cancer may be related to a buildup of estrogen in that gland, not testosterone.

In overweight men, because fat cells convert DHEA and testosterone to estrogen, DIM supplementation can be especially helpful. Michael A. Zeligs, MD, makes the argument that DIM supplementation might improve how the body uses DHEA supplements simply through healthier estrogen metabolism. Recommended dosage: 100 mg per day.

Chrysin

Chrysin blocks the conversion of testosterone into estrogen by inhibiting aromatase. As men age their production of testosterone declines and aromatase increases. Aromatase causes the body to convert testosterone into estrogen, causing an imbalance between these important sex hormones. Many problems result from this including decline in libido, loss of erection, and susceptibility to a number of other nasty health problems including Benign Prostatic Hypertrophy (BPH – enlargement of the prostate).

By inhibiting aromatase, chrysin helps protect what testosterone is already naturally present in your body, preventing its conversion into estrogen. There are a number of in vitro studies which support chrysin's aromatase inhibitory activity. Also, men undergoing testosterone replacement therapy can benefit from decreased conversion of testosterone to estrogen. Recommended dosage: 500 mg per day.

Indole-3-Carbinol (I3C)

Indole-3-Carbinol removes excess estrogen. I3C is a naturally occurring phytonutrient found in cruciferous vegetables (cauliflower, cabbage, cress, bok choy, broccoli). I3C initiates a series of reactions in the body that culminate in the elimination of estrogen. Researchers have observed that metabolism of estrogen occurs via one of two pathways: The 'harmful' metabolic pathway, 16 alpha-hydroxylation, or the 'beneficial' metabolic pathway, 2-hydroxylation. I3C encourages estrogen to take the least harmful path, a process that transforms estrogen into an antiestrogen. Since testosterone converts to estrogen in the male body, eliminating excess estrogen help the male retain as much testosterone as possible, thus increasing libido and strength of erection. Recommended dosage: 100 mg per day.

Sexual Technique Tips

Masturbating Alone or While Your Lover Watches

"If God had intended us not to masturbate, He would have made our arms shorter." George Carlin

Mapping your sexual arousal cycle, learning about your ejaculation response, becoming sensitive to feeling sexual energy build, and learning how to work with it intentionally all require many repetitions of sexual arousal while you observe carefully what is happening inside your body and your thought. Observing and learning these things about your sexual response is possible during intercourse with a partner, but it is much more complex and difficult than learning through self-pleasuring masturbation, or while being pleasured manually or orally by your lover.

There is much unfortunate negative social conditioning associated with masturbation in western culture. Masturbation is often accompanied by feelings of embarrassment, guilt and shame. However, **in eastern sacred sex cultures masturbation is viewed with respect as a most useful method for learning about working intentionally with sexual energy**. A few western authors have written approvingly about the joys and usefulness of masturbation, but this attitude is still quite rare. An excellent example is noted sex-expert Betty Dodson (writing primarily for women) who refers poetically to masturbation as "the ongoing love affair that each of us has with ourselves throughout our lifetime".

Masturbation offers many benefits:

1. You can indulge in any number of self-loving episodes even without a partner. You can have whatever number of repetitions is required to create a sexual arousal map with your arousal scale from one to ten. Masturbation is the most efficient, fastest and easiest way to do this.
2. By repeatedly approaching and backing off from the point of ejaculation, you can learn the split-second timing that is so critical to riding the wave of bliss without going over into the ejaculation response. This is much easier to do without the added dynamics and complexity of intercourse with a partner.
3. You learn to be completely responsible for your own sexual satisfaction.
4. You can determine how and where you like to be touched so you can communicate this information to your lover.

Experiment, take your time and give yourself a very real self-loving exploration as in the Masturbation Ceremony below, not just a quick masturbatory release. Notice how your penis moves through distinct changes before orgasm and ejaculation, he's not just soft and then hard and spewing. Remember, there are **four defined stages of erection:** lengthening and filling; swelling; full erection; rigid erection. The fourth stage, rigid erection, characterized by a penis that's very stiff (a boner) and very hot, signifies ejaculation is close at hand. Through attentive self-arousal or the playful hands and mouth of your sweetheart you can learn how to stay for longer periods of time in the exciting, but less explosive, third stage of firm erection. When you feel yourself moving into the hard, hot level, stop stimulation, relax and pay attention to your breathing. Breathe slowly and deeply.

Masturbation Ceremony

"Don't knock masturbation -- it's sex with someone I love."
Woody Allen

During this masturbation ceremony you will approach your own body with loving tenderness, patience and playfulness. You will treat yourself with reverence and respect. Your purpose is to get to know your erogenous self better, extend your pleasure and endeavor to move your sexual energy. You may end with an ejaculatory orgasm, but that is not your goal.

Set up a sensual space, with a comfy bed or couch, candlelight, sexy music, incense or essential oil diffusers—a sexy space for love. Turn off the phone, lock the door and relax. Allow yourself at least an hour for this magical ritual.

Although this may be unusual for you, begin your loving session by gently stroking and caressing parts of your body other than your genitals—your feet, your neck, the inside of your arms, your face. Start with very light feathery touches with your fingers or a soft cloth or a low-speed vibrator. Arouse your extremities before you move in towards your usual hot spots. Pay attention to the feel of your skin, the line of muscle beneath it, the crinkle of body hair. Take your time and let yourself revel in sensation as you gradually increase the pressure of your touch. You want your whole body to come alive with desire.

Move to your nipples and give them some loving attention with tweaks and twirls. Caress your belly and the insides of your thighs. Go slowly, slowly, teasing yourself, making yourself want more and more just as you'd like your lover to touch you.

Put your fingers in your mouth and suck them gently as you begin to gently fondle your penis. Oil yourself up with lots of good quality lubricant—massaging it into the muscles of your thighs, groin and around your anus as well as along the shaft of your penis. Explore your perineum and anus, with tickles and tender probings. Include some of the acupressure points: groin crease, perineum spot, belly that are illustrated in the section on acupressure p 84.

Pay attention to your testicles—they love to be fondled and admired. Stretch them away from your body as you play. At last begin to give some serious attention to your penis, remembering to take your time and vary the speed, length and pressure of your strokes. With one hand on your penis use the other to tickle your balls, or press your perineum, or insert a finger into your anus. Remember as you are stroking to touch other parts of your body besides your genitals—nipples, belly, ears. Place a palm on your heart center and feel the love you have there for yourself, and for others. Join this love with the sexual desire in your genitals and belly.

Maintain a mental awareness as you love yourself. Map your arousal scale, noticing stages of ejaculation, breath patterns, muscle tightening and so on. Work yourself up to about a 90% level of excitement—when you are highly aroused but not in danger of going over into ejaculation without warning. Then stop stimulation, relax your body, slow your breathing and pay attention to what's happening within. If you need help to slow down try the Penis Tip Squeeze. You can also experiment with the Passion Pump, focusing on circulating your hot sexual energy through your internal orbit. Think about moving your energy through your body away from your genitals, not about stopping ejaculation. **Remember, you get what you pay attention to!** Use your hands to help move the energy by running them in flowing movements from your genitals up your body to your head and above. Make sound as well to send the energy flying.

When your excitement level has dropped begin to stimulate yourself again, slowly bringing yourself up to 90% arousal, then stop and circulate your energy. Do this as many times as you have the time and inclination for. You can end your session with an ejaculation if you choose or simply allow yourself to relax deeply and carry that powerful energy within you. Remember to store it in your belly chakra (two finger widths below your navel). It is safe to hold your sexual energy there.

Complete your self-loving with a restful observation phase. Relax all your muscles, breathe deeply, feel the sensations in every part of your body. Massage your perineum to help disburse any energy still congested there. Finally before you go back to the world give yourself thanks, *aloud*, for such loving pleasure.

Help From Your Partner

Part of opening your heart and being emotionally vulnerable is to be able to ask for what you want. We suggest you communicate clearly with your lover what your desire and intention is with regard to ejaculation. You must let her know that you are starting to learn about delaying ejaculation and that at least sometimes, you want to end lovemaking while you still have desire, i.e., without any ejaculation at all.

You must explain that this does not mean that you are giving anything up. Indeed, you will ultimately experience a great deal more pleasure by ejaculating less. Explain that orgasm and ejaculation are not the same, that you can separate orgasm from ejaculation, and can learn to have multiple orgasms without any ejaculation at all. Also explain how she will benefit from this practice because you will be making love for long enough so she can become fully sexually aroused and awakened and can take all the time she needs and wants to have multiple orgasms. Request that you work most intimately together on learning how to do these things.

It is a common misconception for many women that unless they make their man come, he will not be fully satisfied. You now know that this is, of course, not true. Certainly an ejaculation brings pleasure and this is good, but it also brings a depletion of energy and desire. There is something better than ejaculation and that is multiple orgasms without ejaculation. Any woman who can help her man to have this amazing experience will have a very happy lover.

For Women: Ways To Love Your Man

It is much easier for your man to learn to delay his ejaculation, move his sexual energy and become multi-orgasmic when he takes a passive, **receptive role**. With your loving assistance he'll learn more quickly how to last longer and you'll be the satisfied beneficiary of his increased stamina.

As he is laying back, focusing on keeping his body relaxed, his breathing slow and allowing the energy to spread beyond his genitals, excite him with tender caresses and kisses all over his body. Start from his feet and work up or his head and work down. Tickle and tease, massage and stroke him.

Then focus your attention on his genitals, use your hands or mouth to give him pleasure. Go slow, then fast, varying the speed, pressure and length of your strokes so that he won't reach the point of no-return too quickly. Tantalize him with firm, rapid strokes—use lots of water, oil or silicone lubricant—then switch to slow, gentle cradling. Hold his penis by its happy head and give him a tender shake. Experiment with the 'corkscrew'—sliding your hands down the length of his shaft and twisting lightly as you slide off the end.

Remember to **give attention to other parts**—his testicles, perineum, anus. Pull his balls gently away from his body, stretching the skin of his scrotum sac taut over the testicle inside. With your fingernails lightly scratch the surface—he'll love it!
Move your focus beyond his genitals too—to his nipples, belly, face, legs. You are helping to eroticize all of him. Make eye contact as you stroke and please and tease. Let your partner know with looks, sounds and words that you are enjoying this loving arousal as much as he is.

Be mindful of his arousal signals and when he gets highly excited—for instance if he moves into a stage 4 erection—stop your stimulation. Don't break off your touch but don't make any more movement just yet. Breathe slowly and deeply and encourage him to join your rhythm. Press on his perineum to help him move his sexual energy up and at the same time use your other hand to stroke energy up his torso. You can also employ the Penis Tip Squeeze if he seems very close to ejaculation.

When he has calmed enough—moved back into a stage 1, 2 or 3 erection—begin to arouse him again. Help him climb back up to another peak, then stop stimulation, encourage him to focus on moving his energy and breathing slowly. Repeat this loving process as long as you both want to.

It is also important for you to **be aware of his state of arousal during intercourse**. Remember it is much more difficult for him to back off from the edge when he is the active partner. He'll likely need your help to slow down. This can be hard for you if you are close to orgasm and your body wants to keep going, but it will be well worth the effort in the long run. Instead of continuing to thrust and grind when he is very close to ejaculation, stop your movements and use this opportunity to attempt to move your own sexual energy up from your genitals through your body. When he his excitement level has dropped down you can start your delicious wriggling all over again.

If your partner does have an involuntary ejaculation, celebrate it, don't pout or become annoyed. Show compassion and understanding. If you want more pleasure for yourself ask him to pleasure you, or give yourself an orgasm through masturbation. With practice and attention from both of you, your lover will soon learn how to maintain his erection for significant periods of time.

Anatomy of a Quickie:
Quick Sex Recipe -
Thirty Minutes or Less!

Quick, satisfying sex is one of the great oxymorons of our time. An oxymoron is the juxtaposition of two things that you would not expect to go together—like "biggest little whorehouse in Texas", "virgin birth", "predictable chaos", "random order", "congressional ethics", "progressive conservative", "even odds", "military intelligence", "junk food", and "jumbo shrimp". Our mission impossible assignment, and we decided to accept it, was to come up with a thirty-minute recipe for great sex. Get your stopwatches out. Thirty minutes or less—and it is free—here is the recipe.

Make eye contact. Hold that eye contact. You say something like, "You are gorgeous, completely stunning. I am rendered speechless just looking at your smile. I am so turned on that I can't help myself." Come together kissing—deep French kisses using your tongues. She immediately grabs you by the crotch. You moan, "Oh God!" Your erection is already a major event. She whispers into your ear, "I want you inside me, right now!" Time elapsed: 5 minutes!

You throw her down onto the floor, or swoop her up in your arms and onto a bed or nearby couch, or large padded chair. You jump on top of her in an instant. Tear each other's clothes off. If you have really abandoned yourselves, really let go of all control, you will actually rip and tear them. She takes the tails of your shirt and yanks it open, ripping off several buttons in the process. You pull her skirt up around her hips, grasp her panties in both hands and tear them from her body in one swift action. You are both breathless and growling like animals. Time elapsed: 7 minutes!

Push her bra up around her neck and suck hard on her exposed breasts, cupping them in your hands as you work them, building her desire to a frenzy. Her nipples are hard knobs of excitement. She moans and cries out with the pleasure of it. You whisper in abandoned passion, "I've got to have you. I want you. I love you." She replies, "Yes, yessssss! Please give it to me." Elapsed time: 10 minutes!

She unzips your pants and takes your penis and scrotum full into her hand. You are already on the edge of ejaculating—your excitement is so intense. She pulls your scrotum down from your body, as you scream, "Ahhhhhgggg", a primal animal scream that carries the hot sexual energy up through your body away from your burning, bulging genitals. Her gentle testicle tugging, and your primal animal scream help you delay your ejaculation. Elapsed time: 13 minutes!

You turn around and enclose her erect clitoris in your mouth. She takes your jade stalk into her mouth. You suck in unison. She climaxes instantly and cries out, "Oh yes baby, yessss! Please give it to me. I can't wait another minute." You put your index and middle finger one to two inches insider her yoni, turning them up toward the ceiling and find the G-spot. She climaxes again, deeper this time and more internally, as she writhes and moans in delight. Pre-cum drips from the end of your penis as she now holds it in her hand for caressing and adoration. She licks the clear, odorless, tasteless, deliciously slippery liquid as fast as it is secreted. She knows this is not ejaculate, but an indication of your peak arousal. Elapsed time: 20 minutes!

As you roll over, she settles on top of you, taking you full inside with one swift, incredibly agile move. She gasps at the enormous magnitude of you, and her ejaculate gushes out hotly across your pubic bone, dribbling down to tickle your anus. She begins thrusting rapidly, screaming like a wildcat. Elapsed time: 29 minutes!

She climaxes for the third time as she presses down hard against you, at the same moment reaching down with the index finger of her left hand, and pushing it ruthlessly into your anus. You cum instantly. Sweat covers your bodies as you lie still together—sated, spent, all tension gone, completely at peace, delirious in the safety and comfort of each other's embrace. Elapsed time: 30 minutes!

And now, back to reality—although quick satisfying sex for <u>both</u> partners is not impossible, it is rare. You may think half an hour is not "quick sex", after all according to *Durex' Global Sex Survey 2000* the average time for lovemaking around the world is under 30 minutes, but hey, who wants to be average? When you consider sexual satisfaction, **30 minutes may be plenty of time for a man to get his rocks off but women generally need longer**, especially when making love with a partner. While many women can regularly reach orgasm through masturbation—the Sinclair Sexuality Institute says 60% do—a recent Cosmopolitan survey reports only 18% always find the big O with a lover. Too little time (a diet of practically only fast sex) and lack of technique (i.e., lack of lovemaking skill on the part of the man!) are the big culprits.

Men, especially younger men, seem to enjoy having their genitals touched at any time. This is rarely the case with most women—when a man reaches for breasts or genitals as the <u>first</u> touch it's a turn-off, not a turn-on. That's because **women take much longer than men to come to full arousal**. Remember this one-liner? "Women are ready 15 minutes after men are finished." Although women have as much erectile, pleasure-giving tissue as men, most of it is inside. The woman's clitoris becomes erect and hard as arousal and excitement builds during sexual play. Her inner and outer lips, and the soft tissues at the entrance to the vagina, will become engorged with blood as passion increases. Eventually the entire inside of the vaginal canal will become plump, juicy and sensitized, but it can take as much as an hour or more before she is really ready and eager for penetration. Without proper lubrication of these fragile tissues, intercourse can be unpleasant or downright painful. Even if you use a water-based lubricant, like Astroglide, or Wet, until her vaginal canal is relaxed and open with excitement, penetration won't give her the delightful sensations you'd both like.

Men also find quickies more satisfying than women because they generally enjoy sex at any time. If men make an emotional connection at all, it will be <u>after</u> they have had sex, whereas women often require a heart connection to build their interest. With quick sex aimed at satisfying only her partner's needs a woman may feel she's being used. She may be reminded of a painful experience of sexual abuse, or she may feel guilt and shame based on years of religious and cultural sex-negative conditioning that still says good girls do not really enjoy sex—if they do, they are sluts or whores. Fast sex can bring up this disrespectful imagery, and for women, respect is ultimately important. Fortunately, more women are beginning to claim their right to sexual pleasure as a natural part of a full life, and that includes sexual satisfaction at their pace.

For men, admiration is ultimately important, and admiration from their buddies seems to matter the most—especially for younger men. **Men admire other men who get a lot of sex, and they seem most impressed by the man who gets a lot of fast sex! The more mature a man becomes in his sexuality, the less this will be true—he'll value the opinions of his buddies less, and of his woman more.** Women, especially younger women, are often looking for a committed relationship that will develop and last with great sex as part of it, whereas young men although eager for sex, may rather avoid being tied down in a relationship. For women, loveless sex outside of relationship may make them feel bad about themselves, but for men, sex outside of relationship is an ego-boosting conquest, that confirms they are attractive, desirable and powerful. This difference in perspective leads to very different feelings about fast sex.

This is not to say that women cannot enjoy quickies, they can, but as an occasional experience when the time, energy and feeling is right—for example, if you have been separated for some time. You get back together and jump on each other. Neither of you can wait to even say hello. The whole thing can be over in a few delirious moments. However, it's better—for both of you—if this first quickie is followed by a delicious lingering loving, during which you become intimately reacquainted. Both lovers can also enjoy sex as a way to release tension—fast hot sex is a great way to make up after an argument. Sometimes a woman will take pleasure in fast sex, because she knows it pleases her man, that he really "needed" it to relieve stresses of work or school for instance.

Another scenario in which women honestly enjoy fast sex (as opposed to pretending to or just tolerating it) may be at a party or a bar, where the two of you are complete strangers who make intense eye contact. You approach each other; your pheromones mingle and drive you into an instant, lusty frenzy. As Lou Reed says, "I think it's chemical." There is something about the eyes, the shape of the mouth, the tone of voice, the cut of hair, the exposed cleavage, or the bulge in the pants, that drives you wild in a completely irrational way. You go outside in a dark alley, into your car, or into a storage room and get it on fast and furious. Very few words may have been spoken. You are animals in rut. The danger of it, the excitement of it, the forbiddeness of it, can be so overwhelming that you (especially the woman) act in a way uncharacteristic of your usual behavior.

Speaking of erotic recipes, here is a fun exercise that you can do to get ready for that passionate quickie. Pick any recipe from any cookbook. Add erotica to any part of the recipe to create an erotic poem. Food and poetry are so deliciously erotic! Here is an example to give you the idea.

Tomato-Basil Soup – The Original Recipe

Sauté the onion and garlic in olive oil in a skillet until tender. Add the tomatoes. Cook over medium heat for 10 minutes. Add the tomato sauce, broth, cream, and half of the basil. Simmer for 30 minutes. Process in a blender until smooth. Return to the pan. Add the bread, remaining basil, and Parmesan cheese. Season with salt and pepper. Garnish with additional cheese, oil, and pesto if desired.

Tomato-Basil Erotica or Thirty Minutes Would Never be Enough!

Sauté your lover with onions and garlic,
    thrusting heavy on the garlic.
Rub penis and clit together, drenched in warm olive oil
 until tender but still firm –
"el dente" esta bien!
Sauce it up by spreading overripe tomatoes onto tummies,
using soft circular strokes
slowly at first then speeding up
    sigh and moan to adjust temperature to boiling
    but do not allow penis-Vesuvius to erupt!
Simmer all day and all night, and the next day if desired,
    30 minutes would never be enough.
Blend together, golden rod and fig pocket, like mortar and pestel
    keeping everything smooth.
Turn the heat on and off,
    squeezing the golden rod to add cream
        at the very last moment.

Have fun and take care of each other. Remember, there is nothing wrong with quickies, as long as that is not all you do!

How to Make First Sex Fabulous Sex

The heat is on. You can literally feel it arcing between you. Whether it's an enticing stranger you've just met or a special someone you've been slowly getting to know, you're aware that now is the time to take your connection to the physical level. You can sense that she's about ready to hop into bed and you damn well know that you are. So how do you make this first time with someone new a glorious moment you'll both fondly remember rather than a nightmare you'd just as soon forget?

The first thing to zero in on is attitude. What exactly is it you want from this coming sexual encounter—a lusty one-night romp or the beginning of a longstanding passionate relationship?

There certainly is nothing wrong with a one-night stand. There is something extremely exciting about sex with a stranger, with absolutely no strings attached. Many women feel this way, not only men. What we all have to be careful about is simply using the other person, treating them as an object only for our satisfaction.

No one likes being treated as an object. No one likes being used for someone else's purpose. Men typically use women as sex objects. But just as often women treat men as success objects. What does it mean to treat a person as an object? It means you use that person to get what you want without particular regard to what happens to them or how they feel. At one extreme you would not even care if you actually cause harm. More frequently harm is not intended, but the well being of the person you are using is of little or no concern to you. What is of concern to you is to get what you want, which in this case is sex.

When you want sex and you do anything necessary to get it you are using the woman as a sex object. You may lie and otherwise be deceitful about what is really going on. You may pretend to care or be interested in her, but all you really want is to get laid. After you get what you want, you disappear and she never hears from you again. You don't call. You may not even say hello on the street. You may feel contempt or disgust toward her for having had sex with you. But this is really a disguised form of self-contempt and self-hatred projected onto women. It is very unhealthy and in the long run will leave you alone, lonely, bitter and cynical. This is hardly a prescription for happiness.

Quick sex between consenting adults is not about using each other as an object, assuming both of you understand what is happening, and no deceit is involved. We call this scenario "no-strings sex." With no-strings sex, both parties understand that it is not intended that you will ever see each other again. You do not exchange addresses or phones or personal histories. This situation ranks high on the list of most common fantasy for both men and women. The sex may be extremely hot and passionate. Both lovers may feel an extraordinary freedom and be willing to let go completely, dropping their usual sexual shyness and restraint. Often they will experiment with and allow themselves to enjoy what they would only dream of doing, but never allow themselves to do with someone they knew or were in an ongoing relationship with.

They may experiment with things they did not even dream were possible.

There are only two rules for no-strings sex. They are very simple rules. Rule #1: Mutual consent for everything is mandatory. By "mutual consent" we mean that all aspects of your lovemaking are agreed to by both. You meet together on the sexual playing field as equals. No one gets physically hurt. When your partner says "I don't want to do that" or "stop, that hurts" you must stop instantly. This is where "no" always means no. Rule #2: Don't try to find her later!

The other type of first time encounter is with someone with whom you intend to have an ongoing relationship. We will call this scenario "relationship sex." With relationship sex, it is understood by both of you that there may be an ongoing relationship after the sex. In fact, it would be quite normal for relationship sex to take place after you have been seeing each other for some time. In this scenario sex is not the start of the relationship, but a deepening of it. It is also quite common for a relationship to start with a sexual encounter. If the sex rocks the earth, or even if it is just pretty good, you may want to go further into relationship to see if you can connect on other important levels and make something work together in the longer run. This could evolve into living together or even marriage.

The first rule for no-strings sex also applies to relationship sex. 1. Mutual consent for everything is mandatory. In addition to this rule there are a few others to keep in mind. 2. Great respect is mandatory. 3. Great caring is mandatory. 4. Open, honest communication is mandatory. 5. Gentleness is used as required, and roughness is used as mutually desired.

The Rules

1. Mutual consent for everything is mandatory. If you do not both enjoy it, what is the point? Remember, we are not using each other, we are loving each other. It is certainly all right for one partner to try things because the other person likes it even if they don't, but this is a gift freely given and cannot be required.

2. Great respect is mandatory. Respect implies that you are aware of what the other person wants. You are willing to discover what they are capable of and what their sexual limits are. Your lover may have been injured psychologically or emotionally from past relationships. In fact this will almost certainly be the case, almost everyone has had their heart broken at least once.   At the extreme, they may have experienced sexual abuse as a child. They may feel insecure about their sexuality. They may suffer from low self-esteem as a lover. They may be quite inexperienced in sexual technique. You must be extremely patient and ever so sensitive to the messages they send out about how fast to proceed, what to do and not do. Talk openly to establish the boundaries of your sexuality. Then experiment to push back the boundaries at a pace you can both find comfortable and safe.

3. Great caring is mandatory. Love is always given and received as a gift. It has been said that there is no such thing as bad sex, that sex without love can still be great sex, but sex with caring adds a warmth

that connects two hearts and souls together. This is sex beyond technique. Sex with caring leaves the lovers filled. Sex with love leaves the lovers overflowing. It is caring that moves sex beyond the physical to allow for the creation of a deeper spiritual connection. Most men want an emotional connection and most would welcome a more spiritual experience of sex, but they are afraid and they just haven't learned how to do it yet. Most women quite frankly, require the emotional connection as the price of entry.

4. Gentleness is used as required, and roughness is used as mutually desired. With mutual consent anything goes. But it is usually best to start out with more gentleness and progress to more roughness only as you learn that she wants it and likes it. Many women like a playful roughness as long as they feel truly safe. But if you have not established a high degree of trust with her, roughness prematurely can end what could have been an excellent long-term sexually passionate relationship.

5. Open, honest communication is mandatory. Talk about sex. Tell each other what you like and dislike. A good way to do this is to always offer choices A and B and ask which she likes best. This avoids the damage to fragile egos that young men are so prone to when they are learning about a new lover. If a man hears, "I don't like that" it is very easy for him to have his feelings hurt and this may cause him to withdraw, or get angry, or react in some dysfunctional way. But if you give your women, for example, the choice between fondling her breasts this way, or this way, and ask which is best, you

will not have your feelings hurt, and you will quickly learn what she really likes. This is how a lover becomes a great lover.

If you need to have your imagination stimulated to know what to try, read any of several great lover's manuals available in good bookstores everywhere. Then use the A-or-B technique to find out about your woman specifically.

Once you've honestly considered your attitude you can move into the physical aspects of loving: like the setting, foreplay, afterplay and all the juicy bits in between. In the East there is a long tradition of the warrior lover – a man who has prepared himself physically, emotionally and mentally for the great and glorious battle between the sheets. This is not for dominating or defeating your lover but for skillfully bringing out the best in both of you so you can rise to new heights in your sexuality.

The idea of creating the right ambience for lovemaking may seem artificial or calculated, but there is an art to great loving and why not bring out the artist in yourself? A secluded place, candlelight, music, wine, food and clean sheets may sound like a trite scene from an old James Bond movie but they still hold true. Women love to be adored and creating a special place for loving shows that you care about what they want too.

It has become common knowledge that foreplay is very important in bringing a woman to sexual satisfaction. She takes longer to become aroused to the point where she can match you in intensity of desire. But what is also essential is afterplay. When you've come to a happy climax don't just roll over and go to sleep or get up and go home. Even though your hormones may be telling you you're finished, your lover won't be. Take the time and make the effort to show your appreciation and caring through some tender cuddling and soft words or by sharing some food and conversation. You'll benefit too from staying in love's sweet afterglow.

Finally, it shouldn't have to be said but it still does, always, always practice safer sex. Use condoms and dental dams until you are certain you're in a completely monogamous relationship and you've both had AIDS tests. Remember good first time sex with someone means no one gets hurt, during loving or afterwards.

The Lover's Curse of Memory: How to Be Here Now In Bed

The curse of memory is that memory robs us of being in the moment. We remember the last time we saw something and we see it as we remember it, rather than as it is NOW. We remember how something tasted, and we taste it now as we remember it was. We do the same with all the senses. We hear what we remember having heard before. We smell what we have always smelled. We feel what we felt before. We don't walk up the stairs NOW, we walk up the same stairs we have walked up hundreds or thousands of times before without any awareness of what we are doing. We touch our lover's body from memory. It is not real skin, it is the skin we remember touching hundreds or thousands of times before. And we get bored with our memory. And we hate to be bored. And we want something new. Variety, something new, reawakens our senses. If we touch new skin, we pay attention in a way that makes us aware we are alive. If we smell new pheromones, our nose confirms that we are alive with excitement and arousal. If we taste new wine, our mouth awakens to exhilaration.

The only way most people know how to feel alive is through variety. They have no other strategy to employ. Being in the NOW MOMENT is something you may conclude just happens to you now and again, almost by accident. You may even assume it only happens when you try something for the very first time, or for those exceptional things that are so outstanding and excellent that they can repeatedly transform you into high states of being, for example a favorite selection of music, or intercourse with someone new for say the first 103 times! After that it is memory again and time to move on to someone new! Variety is the spice of life!

But once you learn to consciously, intentionally, deliberately stay in the moment, each moment is unique and new and "as if" for the very first time. In the NOW MOMENT, no matter how many times you have touched, tasted, smelled or seen your lover's skin, it is still as if it were the very first time! One of the tricks to staying in the now moment, is to become aware of how you are running on memory instead of being here now. Running on memory is just like running on empty. That is why it cannot sustain excitement, motivation and passion. There is just not enough juice in memory to keep you going.

Memory is quick to fill in the blanks, or complete the thought, or complete the sensory impression, before the whole has been received and integrated into experience. For example, at the first smell of a familiar body odor, our memory quickly supplies the remainder before the whole of the smell has been registered in our sensory experience. It may remind you of a series of memories associated with that smell when you were a child or at some earlier time in your life. You may find yourself feeling emotions that were associated with that smell. It is this attachment of emotions from memory that makes so much of what we take in with our five senses (hearing, taste, smell, touch, and seeing) positive or negative, good or bad. One thing reminds us of another thing, and before you are aware of it you are off in thought about the past or the future, out of the NOW MOMENT.

But if you really pay attention, you can train yourself to take in information through your senses "as if" for the very first time. When you do this, it is always new, always fresh, always "enough" because you are being in the NOW MOMENT. Confirm for yourself with repeated observations that when you are in the NOW MOMENT you are complete, you are whole, nothing is missing, nothing more needs to be added. Variety is not the spice of life, being here now is!

Here is an incredibly easy but powerfully effective way to rapidly improve the quality of your experience during lovemaking, by helping you get out of memory and get into the Now Moment. With this simple technique, we call the *dial technique*, men can learn to delay ejaculation, women can learn to have multiple orgasms, you can overcome feelings of embarrassment, shame and guilt, win over fear, worry and boredom, you can keep passion and excitement alive in your relationship forever, and you can have lots more fun with your lover.

Neurolinguistic Programming (NLP) is a process of figuring out exactly how your brain does what it does, and then articulating that process in a technique or strategy that you or others can use to accomplish the same end result. Since your brain creates some experiences that are positive and other experiences that are negative, you can use NLP to stop doing what you don't want and start doing more of what you do want. For example, if you know how you make yourself bored during lovemaking, you can stop doing that. If you know how you make yourself excited during lovemaking, you can do more of that.

A key to NLP is the realization that states of being, states of consciousness, and feeling states are not things that just happen to you accidentally, i.e., you are not just a victim of the circumstances of your life. With the **dial technique** you can create a master control panel that displays all the buttons you need to orchestrate your lovemaking into a masterpiece of creativity, joy and ecstasy.

Success with Tantra lovemaking requires that you go out of your mind and get into your body. This means getting out of thought and into sensation.

One form thought takes is memory. Memory is very useful for lots of things, but during lovemaking it can also be a problem. You must learn to differentiate between what kind of memory is helpful and what kind is not helpful. Your body remembering how to do things, for example - keeping internal smooth muscles relaxed during peaks of sexual arousal, is very helpful, because this kind of memory does not mimic thought. But if your memory mimics thought it will put you into your head and keep you out of your body. One of the most pernicious types of memory is the memory of your lover's body, or the memory of how lovemaking has previously progressed step-by-step, as a pattern that you then repeat over and over.

The problem with this type of memory is that you may find yourself making love to a memory rather than a real person, even though that real person is right in bed with you. This naturally leads to very unsatisfying lovemaking and gets boring very quickly. You may find yourself feeling and thinking, "every time we make love is just like every other time we make love". Pretty soon, your lovemaking drops off to almost nothing – no fun, no excitement, no passion, nothing new, and perhaps eventually little or no lovemaking at all, or one or both of you seeks refreshment in an affair.

Sensation refers to the information that comes to you through your senses – sight, sound, smell, taste, feeling (kinesthetic feelings such as heat/pressure, wet/dry, or hot/cold, not emotional feelings such as joy or fear). Great Tantric lovers have learned how to filter out memory (go out of their minds) and how to turn up the intensity of sensation (get into their bodies).

Here is a technique that lovers can use to help them go out of their minds and get into their bodies. It is the *dial technique*. You can find all sorts of interesting variations for using this technique in other areas of your life besides lovemaking. This technique is very simple to use. To apply this technique you simply create in your imagination one dial for whatever you want to diminish and/or another dial for whatever you want to increase.

In your imagination, create one dial that controls your memory (the kind of memory that mimics thought, e.g., remembering how something was the last time you did it), and create another dial that controls sensation. Make the dials different colors, for example the memory dial can be blue (symbolic of thought) and the sensation dial can be red (symbolic for the body). Any colors that feel right for you will work. These are your dials after all. You can also put textures, and other personalized touches to your dials. For example you could cover them with pieces of cloth that you are fond of. You can make the buttons different sizes if you want. For example you might want the sensation dial (or the things you want to increase in intensity) really big and the memory dial (or the things you want to decrease in intensity) really small.

During your lovemaking, find the dials in your imagination and turn the dial for memory way down in intensity, strength, volume, or voltage to nothing at all. At the same time turn the sensation dial way up in intensity, strength, volume, or voltage to a very high level – a level that you are comfortable with. Turning the dials up or down simply means, in your imagination see your hand actually grab the button and turn it. You could also visualize a pointer on a dial screen increasing or decreasing, or the lights on a digital light meter, such as the indicators of a stereo signal on an amplifier, increasing or decreasing as you turn the button. Use any aid to visualization that works for you to show increase or decrease in intensity.

It is important that you don't rush to the maximum intensity of sensation. You don't want to be frightened or feel overwhelmed if such feelings are new for you. Gradually increase the intensity of sensation during successive sessions of lovemaking. Once you have learned to do this you will no longer need to rely on using your buttons. The *dial technique* is only necessary until you have learned to decrease or eliminate what you don't want and increase what you do want in your lovemaking. After that, this process becomes automatic and your lovemaking is permanently transformed.

Be creative in your use of this technique. Here are a few other suggestions for using the *dial technique* during lovemaking.

Here are some examples of buttons you might want to create and then turn down the intensity. These buttons could include any aspect of your lovemaking that you are unhappy with.

fear, quick male ejaculation response, worry, guilt, shame, embarrassment

Here are some examples of buttons you might want to create and then turn up the intensity. These buttons could include any skill, knowledge or feeling that you want to be more present in your lovemaking.

love, general relaxation response, internal smooth muscle relaxation, female orgasm response, female ejaculation orgasm response, joy, fun, playfulness, creativity, comfort

Examples of buttons you might want to turn up if you want more or down if you want less:

danger, excitement (sometimes too much is too much), vulnerability, and so forth.

If you create a lot of buttons be aware of getting yourself confused. It may be wise to use only a few buttons at a time. You might also record the buttons on paper. Draw pictures of the buttons and clearly label them so later you can remember which buttons are for which experiences. Drawing the buttons can also help you more easily visualize them in your imagination. You could also add numbers to the buttons. You could have red1, red2, etc.

Once you have learned how to use this technique, and your lovemaking has been successfully transformed, you will find that every time you make love is like the first time! You will feel that thrill, that excitement, that anticipation, that longing for your lover that you felt the first time you made love with them. In fact it is the first time, because you are not invoking thought/memory to compare it with. This is delightful indeed, and is one of the secrets to staying in love and keeping passion alive in a relationship that lasts a lifetime. This is a key skill necessary to enable you to create love year after year with the same person. This is one important way to keep a monogamous committed relationship hot, sexy, juicy and exciting – indefinitely! Do you use the dial technique? Don't you wish every lover did?

List of Illustrations

About Authors Al Link and Pala Copeland

Al Link and Pala Copeland own and operate 4 Freedoms Relationship Tantra. Since 1987 they have been Tantric lovers and have been teaching others since 1997. They regularly host evening and weekend workshops and occasional weeklong retreats in exotic locations around the planet.

Contact Al and Pala

tantra-sex.com
4freedoms@tantraloving.com

The ***Discovery Channel*** says, "Al and Pala teach couples how to have the best sex of their lives." Discovery Sex Files, "*Better Sex Series*

Books by Al and Pala

Soul Sex: Tantra for Two

Our emphasis in *Soul Sex* is helping couples learn to create love empowering them to thrive for a lifetime together in secure relationship happiness. Discover how to use your relationship as a spiritual practice, and how through it you can know God and serve the world. Thought-provoking discussions, personal stories and simple easy-to-apply practices inspire readers to bring these concepts into their daily lives. The observations and exercises we include are drawn from our own passionate partnership and from the hundreds of couples we have had the privilege to teach at our Tantra sacred sex workshops. Detailed references to books, videos, music and online resources provide readers with opportunities to further explore relationship, sexuality and spirituality.

"*Soul Sex* is a guide for those who want to leave the old western perception of love making behind and shift to the art of divine humans expressing love through the channels of our soul. The authors share an authentic and wholistic view that brings new hope to couples who desire to stretch beyond limitations and move into a more thriving

145

partnership that deepens and brings true connection of union in the soul sex experience." *Claire Papin, Co-host of Wisdom Today Radio Show*

The Complete Idiot's Guide to Supercharged Kama Sutra

The *Kama Sutra* teaches that extraordinary sex is a worthy element of a full and rich life. Everyone deserves the satisfaction of sex that's truly supercharged. And everyone, including you, can learn to make that kind of love. Whether you're a novice in the arts of love or know your way around the bedroom quite well, you'll find ideas and practices that will add spice and satisfaction to your love life. Gorgeous full-color photos show you how!

Sensual Love Secrets for Couples
The Four Freedoms of Body, Mind, Heart & Soul

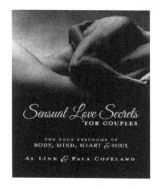

Sensual Love Secrets for Couples offers a simple yet profound idea for stoking the fires of lifelong intimacy: awaken your **body, mind, heart, and soul**. These **four "freedoms"**—the essence of human nature—have the power to transform a partnership into a divine union of desire, pleasure, and lasting love. Unlike other relationship books that focus on problems and how to fix them, *Sensual Love Secrets* reveals how couples can keep a sense of discovery, pleasure, and appreciation alive in a marriage by exploring and engaging each other in discovering and expressing all four freedoms.

Sensual Love Secrets for Couples features over one hundred playful and creative activities designed to help you and your partner establish trust, cultivate emotional intimacy, embrace commitment, open up to pure sexual pleasure, and build spiritual bonds that last a lifetime.

Note: ***Sensual Love Secrets for Couples*** is also available as a downloadable electronic book..

28 Days to Ecstasy for Couples, Tantra Step by Step

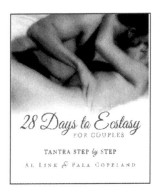

Tantric sex, the art of sacred loving, expands your sexuality beyond the physical. This ancient practice of uniting sex and spirit is especially relevant for modern lovers who long for deeper connection and greater pleasure. This book shows you that Tantra is a practical approach to intimacy that can have a profound impact on your life, without requiring a great deal of extra time.

Tantra Sex Step by Step contains a 28 day plan with simple instructions including fun-to-do activities that will help you re-create your relationship and strengthen your sexual/spiritual bond until it becomes unbreakable. The exercises are quite short—on average you'll spend no more than 20 minutes per day on your sacred loving practice— less time than you may spend watching a TV sitcom or the evening news. Once per week there are longer lovemaking periods in which you reap great delights from the skills you've been learning. By the end of the 28 days you'll have changed your life.

Note: *28 Days to Ecstasy for Couples, Tantra Step by Step* is also available as a downloadable electronic book, entitle *Tantra Sex Step by Step*.

Audio Books by Al and Pala

"The Complete Secrets of Lovemaking"

Multi-media Course includes:

- **227 minutes of mp3 audio**
- **600 pages of pdf text**

We have had three of our electronic books professionally read and digitized into MP3 files that you can listen to on your iPod, your car or home stereo. Listening to these wonderful sacred sexuality guides gives you a completely different perspective than reading them on your computer. You can listen to samples from each of the audio books by visiting **tantra-kama-sutra.com**.

Here are a few teasers about what you will learn when you listen to these audio books.

- Lifetime sexual fitness in just three minutes per day with one simple exercise...
- The secret to finding any woman's g-spot instantly...
- The three ancient secrets for making any women multi-orgasmic...
- Open your heart and really feel love in one minute with this technique...
- Pump up the passion, keep monogamy hot, with the 10-second kiss...

- The one thing about sex you learned in high school that is invaluable now...
- Two simple things men need to learn in order to separate orgasm from ejaculation...
- Three types of orgasms for men, and you can have them all!
- Gain a serious competitive advantage in sports or business over ordinary men who do not know how to do this...
- Four stages of erection and what they mean...
- Breathe this way and delay ejaculation indefinitely...
- Squeeze here at the right time and stop any ejaculation...
- How to have energy orgasms—ooh la la...
- Control is the enemy of ecstasy...
- How to break the sound barrier—sounds to set you free...
- The butterfly pelvic technique...
- How to breathe for deepest intimacy...
- Go out of your mind and get into your body—focus on your senses...
- Stop distracting thoughts that take you out of the lovemaking...
- The sexual fire breath—hot, hot, hot...
- The passion pump—oh my goodness!
- The big draw method for really big orgasms...

eBooks by Al and Pala

100 Ways to Keep Your Lover

100 Ways was our first and remains our most popular eBook

Tantra & Kama Sutra Sex Positions

This is one of three *Kama Sutra* eBooks. Hot! Very sexy!

Kama Sutra Sex Positions and Liberator Shapes

Create some bedroom magic!

Kama Sutra Super Sex

This is the "full monty!"

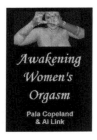

Awakening Women's Orgasm

Say yes to your confident, spiritual, sexy self!

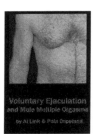

Voluntary Ejaculation & Male Multiple Orgasms

Men, as well as women, can have multiple orgasms!

Sensual Love Secrets for Couples: The Four Freedoms of Body, Mind, Heart & Soul

This is the electronic edition of our published book by the same title.

Tantra Sex Step by Step: 28 Days to Ecstasy for Couples

This is the electronic edition of our published book by *28 Days to Ecstasy for Couples*.

Enlightenment: To Light Within Beyond all Pain and Suffering

One very sticky problem—the illusion of separation. One elegant simple solution. Enlightenment instantly solves every instance of pain and suffering.

Enlightenment for Two Through Sacred Sexual Union

Find the spiritual dimension of Tantra sex, and explore it, using relationship as a spiritual practice leading all the way to "enlightenment for two."

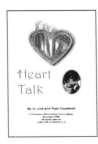

Heart Talk: Relationship Rescue

This is electronic **video book** includes both text and over 30 minutes of video instruction. <u>Solve any relationship problem you have, regardless of how serious you think it is or how long it has been troubling you.</u>

Save up to 40% with our **eBook packages**.
Visit tantra-sex.com

153

Videos by Al and Pala

Tantra Sex Step by Step: Home Study Course on DVD

This 28 day program teaches you the joys of Tantric lovemaking through a full-length video and eBook (the electronic version of our published book). This home study course presents a complete learning curriculum including learning outcomes, questions for review and reflection.

Kama Sutra Super Sex: Home Study Course on DVD
The secrets of the *Kama Sutra* masters are yours with this DVD and eBook home study course. This home study course presents a complete learning curriculum including learning outcomes, questions for review and reflection. .

Videos by Al, Pala, Gaia and Atia

Female Ejaculation: Simple Steps to Sexy Squirting

Atia says "I can teach any woman to ejaculate!"

Other titles featuring Gaia and Atia

- A Woman's Guide to Sex Toys

- The Art of Self Exploration and Pleasure: a Woman's Guide to Masturbation

- Return to the Sacred Waters for Healing and Bliss: Bathing Rituals

CDs from Al and Pala

Apertio: Tantra Energy Meditations

Guided meditations for working with your sexual energy, including the 16 minute sexual fire breath. Pala's voice with music by Jeff Davies.

Workshops and Coaching

Pala and Al host romantic Tantra couples' weekends and weeklong vacation retreats and offer sex and relationship coaching by phone anywhere in the world.

Al Link and Pala Copeland
4freedoms@tantraloving.com
tantra-sex.com

Endnotes

[i] *Dr. Whitaker Wellness Institute Guide To Nutrients*, Julian Whitaker M.D., Summer 1998

[ii] Life Extension Foundation "Male Hormone Modulation Therapy." http://www.lef.org/

[iii] "Boosting Testosterone Levels for Cardiovascular Health", Lane Lenard, Ph.D., "Vitamin Research News", December 1999

[iv] "Testosterone: Not Just For Men," Jane Brody, *Pro Health*, May/June 1998

28825474R00093

Made in the USA
San Bernardino, CA
07 January 2016